the art of
ELOQUENCE

the sacred rhetoric of
Gardner C. Taylor

Joseph Evans

Foreword by Richard Lischer

JUDSON PRESS
PUBLISHERS SINCE 1824
VALLEY FORGE, PA

The Art of Eloquence: The Sacred Rhetoric of Gardner C. Taylor

Interior design by Beth Oberhholtzer.
Cover design by Danny Ellison.

Library of Congress Cataloging-in-Publication Data

Names: Evans, Joseph Claude, author.
Title: The art of eloquence : the sacred rhetoric of Gardner C. Taylor /
   Joseph Evans ; foreword by Richard Lischer.
Identifiers: LCCN 2020003639 (print) | LCCN 2020003640 (ebook) | ISBN
   9780817018146 (paperback) | ISBN 9780817082130 (epub)
Subjects: LCSH: Taylor, Gardner C. | Sermons, American--African American
   authors--History and criticism. | Baptists--Sermons--History and criticism. |
   African American preaching--History--20th century. | Baptists--Clergy--
   Biography. | African American clergy--Biography.
Classification: LCC BX6495.T37 E93 2020 (print) | LCC BX6495.T37 (ebook)
   | DDC 251.0092--dc23
LC record available at https://lccn.loc.gov/2020003639
LC ebook record available at https://lccn.loc.gov/2020003640

Printed in the U.S.A.

First printing, 2020.

In Memory of

Reverend Doctor Thomas Vaughn Walker
Proverbs 18:24

Contents

Foreword
The Great Chain of Preaching

The philosopher of rhetoric Kenneth Burke, who did more to shape our understanding of the "courtship" of speech than anyone in the twentieth century, spoke of rhetoric in all its dimensions as "the Unending Conversation." You and I join that conversation long after it has begun and will leave it long before it is over. But by listening to our forerunners and attending to their wisdom, we may tentatively make our own contributions and thereby help shape the future of the conversation.

Preaching, too, is such an enterprise, and it is closely related to the rhetorical tradition. The Great Chain of Preaching is an arc that spans the centuries. In the words of Psalm 68 in the Great Bible of 1540, "The Lord gave the word: great was the company of the preachers." Like rhetoric, it wasn't invented by us, and we will not be around at its conclusion.

More than anyone in the twentieth century, Gardner C. Taylor embodied both the Unending Conversation and the Great Chain of Preaching. Some believe that rhetorical or homiletical eloquence has gone out of style. If you read the texts and follow the tweets, you might believe it. But listen to a Taylor sermon and you will know that eloquence never went away. Listen to a Taylor sermon and you will find yourself asking, as I often do, how did he do that? And, where does it come from? What secret alchemy produces such a preacher?

No one is better prepared to answer such questions than Dean Joseph Evans, who has gone deeper and further than anyone I know to unravel the "mystery" of Gardner C. Taylor.

By offering a clear and patient exposition of the canons and offices of rhetoric, Evans sheds light on the genius of Taylor. His book is not merely an appreciation of Taylor but an education in Taylor and the traditions that shaped him. These include Taylor's mastery of the three fundamental modes of persuasion: *logos*, or the reasonableness of his argument; *pathos*, the barely contained suffering and joy of his soaring baritone; and *ethos*, which in the classical tradition meant "the good man speaking well," and for early Christian preachers, a great man of humility and prayer.

Evans also traces Taylor's mastery of the offices of rhetoric, including the discovery of ideas, their arrangement, style, memory (the most neglected skill), and delivery. He shows how these and many other talents were mediated to Taylor through his engagement with the Scottish belles lettres tradition of the eighteenth century; the Elocution Movement of the nineteenth century; pulpit greats, such as Alexander Maclaren, F. W. Robertson, and Charles Spurgeon; as well as "Black Victorian" ideology, the Harlem Renaissance, and other fertile incubators of eloquence. But perhaps the greatest of all influences was Gardner Taylor's special life, begun in rural Louisiana and consummated amidst the trials and joys of Brooklyn, New York. Understanding the influences on Taylor is helpful to us all, but there is no formula for making another like him.

I am most grateful for the ways in which Evans displays Taylor's transformation of classical rhetorical. He did not merely adapt rhetoric to the gospel of Jesus Christ any more than Augustine did so in his sermons. In the act of preaching, rhetoric is reborn as a servant, not a master. No one will say of a Taylor sermon that it was "just" rhetoric, for the classic techniques—and there were many— are always veiled by the splendor of God's written word and the mercy of Christ's redeeming sacrifice. All of which leads to a final note on ethos: classical orators were not known for their humility, but because Taylor received the gift of preaching and understood its magnitude, his was an eloquence graced by humility.

Many of us have forgotten Augustine's comments on the sermon's three purposes: to teach, to delight, and to move. Evans' book offers a gentle corrective to sermons that are satisfied with "delight," that is, entertainment, and go no further. He invites us to follow the discipline of eloquence to a better place at which hearts are moved and lives are changed.

I learned much from this wise book, not only about its main subject, but about myself and my own attempts to preach. If other readers are similarly instructed and moved, Evans' book has a long and blessed future.

Richard Lischer
James T. and Alice Mead Cleland Professor
Emeritus of Preaching
Duke Divinity School

1

An Introduction to the Art of Eloquence

The road to eloquence is a hard road and a lonely road, and the journey is not for the faint-hearted. —Edward P. J. Corbett and Robert J. Connors

ardner Taylor is considered one of the most eloquent preach-ers of the twentieth century, and by the century's end, his image was chiseled into the Mount Rushmore of elite preachers alongside Mordecai Wyatt Johnson, Vernon Napoleon Johns, Benjamin Elijah Mays, Howard Washington Thurman, Samuel DeWitt Proctor and Martin Luther King Jr.[1] Taylor was well-known in African American church circles for decades. He was prominent in black Baptist denominational wars and had the psychic bruises to prove it.[2] It was in the 1990s, however, that Taylor emerged into the mainstream's national consciousness. Later in this book, we will reinforce this statement when we consider Taylor's homily "Facing Facts with Faith," which was delivered during the inaugural prayer service of William Jefferson Clinton in Washington, DC, on January 20, 1993.[3]

During that same period, a sermon whisperer, Richard Lischer, made the following remarks about Taylor's pulpit oratory, rightly pointing toward what we describe as the penultimate symbol of the so-called liberal Protestant preaching tradition. Lischer wrote that Taylor's oratory was an "inventory of African-American pulpit rhetoric—understatement, the ponderous ingratiation, parallelism, antithesis, the prophetic

1

stutter, peroration, and the adroit manipulation of thematic set pieces all delivered in a voice like a pipe organ."[4] Lischer is correct. Taylor's oratory made him a standard bearer within his hallmark tradition. However, Taylor's preaching prowess became distinctly more broadly known after his participation in Clinton's inauguration.

Taylor's pulpit work was filled with an artist's distinctive that made his rhetoric powerful and unforgettable. Rhetoric has many definitions, but here we define rhetoric as the foremost art of persuasion.[5] In a narrower manner, we emphasize the art of eloquence which informs rhetoric and is at the center of persuasion. It was Taylor's mastery of the art of eloquence, his use of that art, which became the foci of his narrative form. This assertion, we contend, makes the art of eloquence more comprehensible.

Indeed, the art of eloquence is Taylor's peculiar manner. His eloquence then transcends theological boundaries and sociopolitical and cultural constructs. His crafted sacred rhetoric is simply beautiful to hear. Taylor's sacred rhetoric then belongs to the ages because he mastered the ancient art of eloquence. It is his signature, and it sets his sermon craft uniquely apart. For this, and for nearly a century, he stands firmly as an eminent pulpiteer. Taylor's eloquence shapes his narrative's contours and boundaries as a frame complements a portrait mounted in an exclusive art gallery.

This is the art of eloquence. Eloquence, one of the five canons of rhetoric (hereafter referred to as elements of rhetoric), is our focus because we have determined that it is the predominate canon that informs Taylor's rhetoric. Taylor's peculiar manner may be located among the most erudite statesmen, politicians, and lawyers—which Taylor could have become. Instead, Taylor's erudite rhetoric is attached to the work of a preacher who labors over biblical texts.[6] In short, Taylor's biblical worldview informed his employment of the art of eloquence and more broadly his rhetoric. Taylor's oratory then can be characterized as a part of a sacred rhetoric tradition.

In this way, we are interested in how eloquence functions and intersects with the other elements of rhetoric (invention, discovery, style, memory, and delivery). Of a second import, which we shall see later, Taylor shares with Frederick Douglass and Martin Luther King Jr. an innate ability and instinct to use the art of eloquence in order to paint word pictures which shape contours and rhetorical boundaries that are important for building a narrative. Though we contend that Taylor shares the art of eloquence with these other luminaries, we further contend that Taylor's art of eloquence rises above Douglass's and King's adaptations because Taylor's eloquence is so firmly attached to his peculiar manner, that is, how he preached biblical texts.

An example of Taylor's art of eloquence is located in his sacred rhetoric or what is more commonly known to readers as a sermon narrative: "Seeing Our Hurts with God's Eyes" (John 15:1). With proper word choice, word organization, and arrangement, Taylor captures Jesus' countenance while he is in the company of his anxiety-ridden disciples. The scene refers to that which took place on the eve of Jesus' crucifixion. "He's talking . . . about deep and intimate things, [he] unburdens his heart . . . seeking to rally them against the chill . . . and the indignities . . . He tells them . . . the most tender [words] he ever uttered."[7]

Taylor's art of eloquence adds powerful clarity to his narrative, which describes what is known as the scene of the Last Supper in the upper room. He avoids inordinacies; his sacred rhetoric employs words that are common to most people; it is effective; it is commanding because he has used balanced pure words that are symmetrical in their arrangement. His sacred rhetoric is nonviolent, nonthreatening, and inoffensive. Taylor's sacred rhetoric is the paint, brush, and canvas that he uses to craft his art of eloquence.[8]

Taylor paints a picture of the scene around the first Maundy Thursday Communion. His word pictures are like a mirror that provides a full reflection of what it means to be human and what it means to be human under heavy burdens. In short, it reflects what is common to all. When we see our reflection, we see our similar uncertainties that await us. Taylor's transparency speaks to his credibility, which Aristotle calls character or ethos. In Aristotle's definition, "character (ethos) is the most potent of all means of persuasion."[9]

It matters then who is doing the persuading; that is, can that person be trusted? What is more, Taylor is trusted to be eloquent; this is how he establishes his character or ethos. In short, Taylor's art of eloquence is what his audiences have come to expect and have come to hear. It is his eloquence that can be interpreted as his embodiment of where the culture, human experience, and biblical texts intersect. As Lischer comments, "Taylor is not so much a storyteller as an incisive and exciting performer of the text and a commentator on the state of the human soul."[10] What is clear and consistent is that Taylor's art of eloquence rises above his use of all other elements of rhetoric.

It is Taylor's art of eloquence that unlocks the hidden door, and we now have a glimpse of how his narrative emerges on a canvas. Like an artist who uses specific paints and brushes to cover a canvas, Taylor similarly uses word choices and word arrangements to paint his narrative. Those who came to hear Taylor were a part of a transformative experience; they became his living and breathing canvas. One writer describes this phenomenon: "Hearing Dr. Taylor preach opens a window to the essence of his soul. There we gain a glimpse of how his character has been wedded to the text."[11]

In order to learn, understand, and perhaps employ the art of eloquence, it must be an intentional effort and practice for preachers. However, we can begin. Our thesis is simple: *We agree that over time, the art of eloquence will only enhance our efforts to improve our narrative development and that a well-crafted narrative persuades.*[12] It is our objective here to present the art of eloquence as Taylor's peculiar manner, a manner that some will choose to add its worth to their sermon craftsmanship.

Thus, we must broaden its terrain to inspire as many preachers as we possibly can. We make this attempt for preachers who seek its many potential benefits. One of those benefits is to make our sacred rhetoric consequential and appealing to our audiences and congregations. Let us add that we intend to be consistent with our interest in eloquence and to demonstrate how eloquence functions and intersects with the other elements of rhetoric and how it informs sacred rhetoric, which enhances our sacred rhetoric narratives. Finally, we will try to be consistent with our claim that the art of eloquence is located predominately in Taylor's approach to his pulpit task and assignment.

What lies at the taproot of sacred rhetoric then is the art of eloquence. Eloquence can be studied and learned on a road less traveled. The road to eloquence indeed is a hard and a lonely road because it takes time to learn how to use it. It is rewarding, but it requires a lifetime commitment to refining it. In short, eloquence is a part of an advanced orator's well-crafted style.[13] What follows is our attempt to polish our argument. That is, we will provide a sharper definition of what we mean by eloquence. Let us begin, then, with comments on how eloquence functions.

How Eloquence Functions

Eloquence functions as persuasion and persuasion as argument. We describe persuasion here as the polish that a craftsperson applies over one's steely, solid, well-structured, and well-crafted argument. Persuasion is what makes an argument smooth and shiny. In this way, persuasion is an argument's veneer. It enhances the substance of an argument, making it attractive and appealing to an audience. The best orators have developed and deployed persuasion to make such an argument. Eloquence that appears as persuasion creates space to reinforce an orator's argument. Eloquence by way of persuasion shapes the contours of an argument upon which orators may stand.

Thus far, we have suggested that eloquence can be expressed as persuasion and persuasion as argument. To restate, a persuasive argument is shiny and attractive. In order for argument to be persuasive, it has subparts which we call helpers or appeals. We call these appeals ethos, logos, and pathos.

Ethos (Credibility or Character)

For now we will describe ethos as credibility or character. What immediately conjures in our minds may be an image of Abraham Lincoln while he stood to deliver the Gettysburg Address. Lincoln made an appeal to his audience that it should demonstrate reverent solemnity toward the sacrifices of the fallen, inviting his audience to consider the character of the memorialized soldiers: "The brave men, living and dead, who struggled here, have consecrated it, far above our poor power to add or detract. The world will little note, nor long remember what we say here, but it can never forget what they did here."[14]

Lincoln pointed to the character of those who fought on the Gettysburg battlefield, but his address could not have been delivered by a person with a character less respected than that of Lincoln. Whether this was understood at the time continues to be debated. It is not debated, however, that a person with a character less respected than that of Lincoln would have been unqualified to deliver the address with his effectiveness. What is more, Lincoln grounded his address in civic religious tones, pointing his audience toward the character or ethos of God: "this nation, under God, shall have a new birth of freedom—and that government of the people, by the people, for the people, shall not perish from the earth."[15]

Lincoln appealed to a universal and widely accepted claim that Otherness is morally incorruptible, but only a person who is believed to be of sound and goodly character (such as Lincoln) is permitted to be associated with such a claim. Therefore, his claim is heard as tasteful, appropriate, and accepted. Otherness is morally incorruptible, and God's character was imputed upon Lincoln and became his moral and ethical justification for him to speak *ex cathedra*.

Logos (Reason)

Second, an appeal to reason is understood as logos. Readers will recall from their literature or civics classes the Athenian scholar Socrates, who was accused of being an atheist and was alleged to have imposed his corrupted ideas upon Athenian youthful minds. In order to refute these charges, Socrates spoke with deliberate, organized, and arranged words to demonstrate his innocence: "I believe in spiritual agencies—so you swear in your affidavit; and yet if I believe in divine things, how can I help believing in spirits or demigods;—must I not?" Socrates defended himself well. He provided an organized and carefully arranged disposition.

Of course, Socrates's defense did not result in his acquittal. Instead, his logical facts led to and revealed truth through his logical method. Truth inflamed the emotions of his accusers. They were ashamed that their guilt, jealousies, and envies against Socrates came to light. In a later chapter, Socrates's use of examples is defined more broadly. What is important here is that we have an example of an appeal to reason. In Socrates's case, however, his reason may have lacked emotion. That is, passion is a necessary appeal or helper to persuade human motives.

Pathos (Emotion)

Therefore, and third, it is necessary to employ pathos or what can be thought of as an emotional appeal. Perhaps what rises into our minds is an image of Harper Lee's fictional character Atticus Finch, the small-town attorney in *To Kill a Mockingbird*. We see Atticus Finch wearing his horned-rimmed glasses and his khaki suit, standing in a steamy courtroom where he delivers one of literature's iconic closing arguments. In his defense of a Negro, a man accused of rape in the early twentieth-century American South, Finch passionately made an emotional appeal for an acquittal: "The defendant is not guilty, but somebody in this courtroom is." And so a quiet, humble, respectable Negro, who has had the unmitigated temerity to 'feel sorry' for a white woman, has had to put his word against two white people's.[16]

Indeed, there was someone sitting in that fictional courtroom who was guilty of rape. However, that man was not convicted by an ethically unconscious jury. It was Finch's client whom the jury found guilty. Although he doubted the jury's capacity to render a not-guilty verdict, Finch made a persuasive emotional appeal. The art of eloquence alone cannot make people morally whole. On the contrary, too often the art of eloquence reveals our deliberate avoidance of wholeness.

What is necessary to add here is that Lincoln's ethos, logos, and pathos did not stop the continuance of the pale, full-throated grave that was the American civil war. Rather, the Confederacy became more strenuously recalcitrant. Socrates's ethos, logos, and perhaps constrained pathos did not change the emotions of his detractors; once again it revealed their insecurities that led to their rage against the Athenian intellectual. Certainly Atticus Finch is a character Lee used to demonstrate that ethos, logos, and pathos do not immediately or possibly ever change the motivations of people. What is important is that in a democracy, human protests and actions have demanded space for truth to be claimed in public squares and public spheres.

In each instance, we have illustrated how an argument's helpers function in context. Lincoln's ethos served as an example of what the national ethos should be; however, that remains a goal that we must achieve. Socrates's appeal was logical, methodical, and deliberate; he chose and arranged his words carefully, as each word was used to build an organized appeal as a part of his reasonable defense. Finch's rhetoric was an appeal that grew out of cultural predisposition and preunderstanding. His passion for justice was made by an emotional appeal, an appeal that called forth justice in a place where injustice was the cultural norm against otherness—and in this instance, otherness was the black male.

An Appreciation for the Art of Eloquence

The next paragraphs serve as preparatory stair steps to a larger picture and an appreciation for the art of eloquence. Let us remember that the art of eloquence is reinforced by persuasion and persuasion by argument. We see an intersection between eloquence, persuasion, and argument's helpers, ethos, logos, and pathos—ways to build, support, and reinforce argument. First, we focus on Lane Cooper's magnum opus, *The Rhetoric of Aristotle* (1932). Cooper's book remains an indispensable work for those who seek an understanding of the art of eloquence. On the subject, Cooper's insight and translation of Aristotle's rhetoric remain respected by those privileged to engage the work in formal study. (Cooper and other scholars we will study use masculine pronouns, a usage that reflects their historical context. We, however, consider the principles espoused by these authors to be gender inclusive.) Thus, we find that Cooper's translation suggests that persuasion depends on the significant role that ethos or character has in understanding the power of persuasion:

> The character of the speaker is a cause of persuasion when the speech is so uttered as to make him worthy of belief; for as a rule we trust men of probity more, and more quickly, about things in general, while on points outside the realm of exact knowledge, where opinion is divided, we trust them absolutely. This trust, however, should be created by the speech itself, and not left to depend upon an antecedent impression that the speaker is this or that kind of man. It is not true, as some writers on the art maintain, that the probity of the speaker contributes nothing to his persuasiveness; on the contrary, we must almost affirm that his character is the most potent of all the means to persuasion.[17]

We notice that Aristotle made mention of "probity," another way to describe integrity and correctness. These have a natural influence upon an audience's expectation of an orator. Lincoln, Socrates, Finch, and Taylor are the kinds of persons who will not avoid controversial and current issues, but such persons will address malignant issues directly. They choose the art of eloquence to deliver the truth.

Of course, a persuasive argument that addresses human-made malignancies will surface malignant opinions. We know that opinions form varied responses that will cause divisions to form among people. However, what is taken into consideration is the character of the orator: "we trust them absolutely"; the orator's "probity." As mentioned, this does not mean that an orator's character and his or her sacred rhetoric will not cause debate and division. This is a cardinal reason why we encourage that all learn the art of eloquence and how it functions as persuasion for preparation of an argument.

We employ the art of eloquence and its helpers in order to prepare our argument in such a way that we are able to refute uninformed opinions that may cause undesirable division in our argument's claims. We shape the contours and boundaries of our argument beforehand; we anticipate dissenters; and we determine beforehand what are our argument's strengths and liabilities. This is a mark of ethos or character. People then are persuaded by the character of the individual in part because character or ethos points toward a record where the orator's consistency is noted. In part, an orator's character and content are trusted because of that person's well-known dogged pursuit of our shared causes. However, an audience has a responsibility to make judgments of our argument in part because their judgment is based upon our argument's plausibility.

Of logos, Cooper references this helper as proofs. According to Aristotle, there are two kinds of proofs: artistic and non-artistic. We might call them scientific and non-scientific. Aristotle distinguishes means of persuasion that inherently belong in art and those that, while associated with it, are eternal and unplanned. We present these as examples:

> Proofs [persuasion] are of two kinds, artistic and non-artistic. By "non-artistic" proofs are meant all such as are not supplied by our own efforts, but existed beforehand, such as witnesses, admissions,

under torture, written in contracts and the like. By "artistic" proofs are meant those that may be furnished by the method of Rhetoric through our own efforts. The first sort have only to be used; the second have to be found.[18]

Let us make further mention about the significant role that proofs have in forming a coherent argument. An artistic proof is something that we know as creative or imaginative, such as illustrations that invite us to think in larger ways. The second, a non-artistic proof, is something that we know to be concrete, such as witnesses, admissions, or contracts. For an example, we return to Taylor's sermon "Seeing Our Hurts with God's Eyes." We will notice that he employs both forms of proofs in tandem:

> Perhaps in thinking about our hurts we attach too much importance to what happens to us rather than looking at the results of the things that happen to us, for what is really grievous is not what happens but how it affects us. That is the meaning of panic, too, of not knowing what to do under this circumstance or under that, of feeling caged, trapped, cornered, helpless. Here is the difference, I am sure, between how a Christian views the things that happen in his or her life and how the person who is not a Christian views the things that happen in his or her life. . . . For the Lord makes his rain fall as he does his sun to shine upon the just as well as the unjust. But there is a difference with which the righteous and the unrighteous receive the rain.
>
> The unrighteous farmer, seeing rain fall when it is needed, is likely to figure it was about time. The unrighteous, to some extent at least, complains. A righteous farmer is likely to look up to the heavens and thank God that the rain came.[19]

As we stated, the preceding excerpt illustrates an intersection between artistic and non-artistic proofs. In this sermon narrative, Taylor begins with a declarative sentence: "Perhaps in thinking about our hurts we attach too much importance to what happens to us rather than looking at the results of the things that happen to us, for what is really grievous is not what happens but how it affects us." Here, Taylor brilliantly and subtly presents his sermon's thesis. Simultaneously, he has provided an artistic proof: "That is the meaning of panic, too, of not knowing what to do under this circumstance or under that, of feeling caged, trapped, cornered, helpless." This gets to what forms our worldview. That is, Taylor expresses that worldview informs how we interpret and understand human experiences.

What follows is an example of a non-artistic proof: "Here is the difference, I am sure, between how a Christian views the things that happen in his or her life and how the person who is not a Christian views the things that happen in his or her life. It is not that the same things do not happen; it is that in a Christian spirit, they are seen in a different way." Here Taylor attempts to move his audience beyond an emotional response toward consideration of a reasonable or rational explanation. In order to help his audience ground his claim, Taylor provides an illustration in which we can locate both an artistic and non-artistic intersection: "The unrighteous farmer, seeing rain fall . . . is likely to figure it was about time. The unrighteous [farmer] . . . complains. A righteous farmer is likely to look . . . and thank God that the rain came." Here we see an example of how these two kinds of proofs are employed in sacred rhetoric.

There is a third subpart of an argument. We call this helper pathos. Cooper translates Aristotle's definition of emotion or pathos throughout his treatises of rhetoric, but for now, the following brief definition is appropriate: "Persuasion is effected through the audience, when they are brought by the speech into a state of emotion; for we give very different decisions under the sway of pain or joy, and liking or hatred. This, we contend, is the sole aspect of the art with which technical writers of the day have tried to deal."[20]

In a later chapter, we shall underline the larger role that pathos has in helping an orator make an emotional appeal in a persuasive argument. What is significant here is that an orator must understand an audience's full range of emotions. A "state of emotion" can point toward what an orator must predetermine about the predisposition and even prejudices of her or his audience. That is, some people are biased emotionally about a certain subject. Some may attend a particular public address to affirm the orator's argument. Still others may attend the same address to distract, while others attend to refute the claim and do so by making false claims about the character of the speaker.

Atticus Finch, for example, understood predetermined emotions that surrounded him in Harper Lee's fictional courtroom. Lee's Finch lived among racist citizens who would make the Negro man the bane of their pitiful conditions. By accusing him falsely, it became easier to convict an innocent man than to admit that their poverty was the real cause of their frustrations, insecurities, and ignorance. Finch knew that the presence of otherness—that is, the utilitarian trope—was the Negro. He became the blame and pleasure, an allegory and an allusion for the impoverished white citizens' imagination and for their visible collective, social, and economic cultural lag. Finch's argumentative goal then was to bend their emotions with truth in order to receive an acquittal for the accused. Like Socrates, who made an appeal for his own acquittal, Finch too was unsuccessful. Finch was not able to make the citizens publically admit their misguided emotions. However, Finch was aware of the state of emotions in his audience.

The Art of Eloquence: Influences upon Taylor, King, and Douglass

Earlier in this chapter, we pointed out certain similarities that link Gardner Taylor, Frederick Douglass, and Martin Luther King Jr. Neither Taylor nor Douglass was trained formally in the art of eloquence. Although Taylor's official transcript from Oberlin College (1937–1940) states that he did take two formal courses in preaching and one formal course in public speaking, Taylor may have not considered public speaking to be a formal course in rhetoric.[21] However, Martin Luther King Jr. studied rhetoric formally.

The exercise began while King was a teenager. His first rhetoric teacher was Gladstone Louis Chandler, who instructed King with his preferred text, *Fundamentals of Public Speaking.*[22] As a seminarian, King continued his rhetorical studies, which included numerous courses in homiletics and Scottish belles lettres, courses that could have enhanced his native genius in sacred rhetoric and his use of the art form on the public platform and in the sacred pulpit.[23] By contrast, Douglass claimed that he learned much about the art of eloquence by his thorough study of Caleb Bingham's *The Columbi-*

an Orator, a book of iconic speeches that affirmed, even demanded, freedom and democracy.

Douglass described his reading of "Dialogue between a Master and Slave," which is an essay included in *The Columbian Orator*, as the progenitor of his personal stride toward liberation:

> I was now about twelve years old, and the thought of being a slave for life began to bear heavily upon my heart. Just about this time, I got hold of a book entitled, "The Columbian Orator." Every opportunity I got, I used to read the book. Among much of other interesting matter, I found in it a dialogue between a master and his slave. The slave was represented as having run away from his master three times. The dialogue represented the conversation which took place between them, when the slave was retaken the third time. In this dialogue, the whole argument in behalf of slavery was brought forward by the master, all of which was disposed of by the slave. The slave was made to say some very smart as well as impressive things in reply to his master—things which had the desired though unexpected effect; for the conversation resulted in the voluntary emancipation of the slave on the part of the master.[24]

Douglass refers to the "Dialogue between a Master and Slave" as a primary source that inspired his awakenings of liberation. The author's personal identity remains anonymous, perhaps to protect her or him from severe violence, but the essay is among the finest apologetic defenses against depraved cultural norms, values, and religious mythologies.

The following passages demonstrate the art of eloquence shared between the anonymous writer of the "Dialogue between a Master and Slave" and Frederick Douglass, the writer and orator of "What to the Slave Is the Fourth of July?" The anonymous writer demonstrates that she or he understands the underbelly of oppression. Douglass shapes a similar narrative which is highlighted before "more than 500 people gathered at Corinthian Hall in Rochester, New York, on 5 July 1852."[25]

"Dialogue between a Master and Slave":
Humane! Does it deserve that appellation to keep your fellow men in forced subjection, deprived of all exercise of their freewill, liable to all injuries that your own caprice, or the brutality of your overseers,

13

may heap on them, and devoted, soul and body, only to your pleasure and emolument? Can gratitude take place between creatures in such a state, and the tyrant who holds them in it? Look at these limbs; are they not those of a man? Think that I have the spirit of a man too.[26]

"What to the Slave Is the Fourth of July?":

What, to the American slave, is your 4th of July? I answer: day that reveals to him, more than all other days in the year, the gross injustice and cruelty to which he is the constant victim. To him, your celebration is a sham; our boasted liberty, an unholy license; your national greatness, swelling vanity; your sounds of rejoicing are empty and heartless; your denunciation of tyrants, brass fronted impudence; your shouts of liberty and equality, hollow mockery; your prayers and hymns, your sermons and thanksgiving, with all your religious parade, and solemnity, are to him, mere bombast, fraud, deception, impiety, and hypocrisy—a thin veil to cover crimes which would disgrace a nation of savages. There is not a nation on the earth guilty of practices more shocking and bloody, than are the people of these United States, at this very hour.[27]

These essays underline dialectic; each characterizes a liberation motif. Douglass rightly was stimulated by the possibility that black human bodies could be liberated from the dreaded nightmare that bondage spawned, a bondage that was sanctioned by the land's government.

Taylor's formal study of rhetoric is questionable. However, while enrolled at Oberlin, Taylor read the literary works of Heywood Broun, a brilliant sportswriter, and Walter Lippmann, a bold political opinion writer.[28] Alongside these journalists, Taylor read numerous sermons from the Victorian era.[29] He was particularly attracted to nineteenth-century pulpit luminaries such as Alexander Maclaren, F. W. Robertson, Leslie Weatherhead, Clarence Macartney, and Charles Spurgeon.[30]

It is noteworthy to provide further context to what Victorianism meant to people of African descent in America. Jeffrey C. Stewart, author of *The New Negro: The Life of Alain Locke*, characterizes Victorianism and its influence on Locke and other people of African descent at the turn of twentieth century:

Ishmael's [Locke's father] faith that culture and accomplishment could triumph over racism lay in the Black Victorian ideology of educated

14

African Americans that held sway for over a century. "Victorianism" came to be the term used for a set of rules for public and private life that characterized middle-class status. On the one hand, sexual prudishness, verbal and literary censorship, and personal self-discipline signified that one was civilized . . . a Victorian style had crystallized into public pedagogy of how the lower and working classes, and minorities and colonials, ought to act if they wanted to be considered middle class and civilized. . . . Victorianism abroad created desire in the subject populations to emulate British culture to gain admission to civilization. Something like that psychology operated among Black Victorians, who inhabited London, Boston, Washington, DC, and especially Philadelphia, where increasingly, educated free Negroes grew up imbibing the nineteenth century's Anglo-American love of class, home, and strict public behavior.[31]

The Victorian era became synonymously known with the reign of Queen Victoria of England. As an eighteen-year-old, her sovereign rule began in 1837 and ended in 1901. Locke was born on September 13, 1885, into an ambitious Philadelphia family—a black Victorian family. In 1901, Locke was sixteen years of age. By then Locke was engaged willingly in his family's expectations. That is, he was conditioned into the black Victorian tradition, a tradition that demanded that he would become an educated professional and that he would uphold his family's so-called class privilege.

In short, his family's expectations of his achievements would reflect "a sense that educated Negroes were at least the equals of their White peers in their mastery of English literature, religious doctrine, and Victorian mores and manners pervaded Black aristocracy, as they sought to call themselves."[32] Although Locke died on June 9, 1954, black Victorianism continued among elite people of African descent and evolved into the culture of Negro respectability. In the 1990s, we witnessed black Victorianism's once invisible presence become visible in *The Cosby Show*. In this popular situation comedy, Cliff Huxtable and Claire Huxtable, a physician and an attorney, raised their family with black Victorian values. Perhaps for the first time, millions of whites and blacks became aware of the possibilities that people of African descent had earned and achieved upper-middle-class social standing and that black Victorianism continued to exist and function.

Prior to Taylor's arrival at Oberlin, it is plausible that he had been exposed to a similar hybrid of black Victorian ideology. For no other reason than to survive hegemonic hostility, black Victorianism had taken root among aspiring blacks. Families like Locke's intentionally appropriated black Victorianism in order to assimilate into America's dominant culture. Black Victorians were considered compliant accomplices and were highly educated, cultured, and westerly civilized. It is quite possible that Taylor may have been predisposed pedagogically to this worldview, and therefore it was his family's and benefactor's expectation for him to pursue a similar course.

What is certain is that while at Oberlin, Taylor studied copiously Victorian-era sermons alongside contemporary works like those of Broun and Lippmann. He more than likely noticed that their composition and rhetoric intersected with that of the Victorian preachers; theirs was a similarly shared rhetorical form and structure. Indeed, there remains a thematic thread. That is, composition and rhetoric shape all narrative form, and Taylor appropriated this style, making it his own in order to craft his art of eloquence that shaped his sacred rhetoric. Thus, we suppose that Taylor's black Victorian predisposition and pedagogy provided for him intellectual space to ground his voice in Victorianism. From this nexus sprang Taylor's mastery of the art of eloquence.

Conclusion

Let us restate our thesis: *We agree that over time, the art of eloquence will only enhance our efforts to improve our narrative development and that a well-crafted narrative persuades.* We further restate that Taylor's art of eloquence informed his sacred rhetoric and shaped the contours of his sermons:

> One pondering a sermon ought to look at the text in its setting and surroundings. A wise preacher of another generation suggested that one ought to "walk up and down the street on which a text lives." The surrounding terrain ought to be taken into account. What is the block like on which the text is located? Is it a rundown section, or does it sparkle with a neat tidiness? Is the sky overhead leaden or gray, or is it bright and sunlit? Does one hear light and merry music in the neigh-

borhood of the text or are there solemn cadences of some sad and mournful time? One need not get lost in atmosphere, but a sense of climate will greatly aid the sermon in breathing with life and having, therefore, an interest in people.[33]

We notice that Taylor's art of eloquence shapes the boundaries of his narrative discourse. He accomplishes this with his careful word choices, and in addition, his words are carefully organized and arranged. In this way, Taylor uses his words to present facts, or what we have called artistic and non-artistic proofs. These helpers are a part of the argument's veneer that makes it attractive and shiny. What Taylor posits is similar to Frederick Douglass's approach. Douglass's narrative form is used to present facts and to place them into evidence. We see this clearly by taking notice of Jacqueline Bacon's careful analysis of how Douglass shapes his narrative form:

> Maintaining his ostensible emphasis on narration, Douglass marshals two strategies that allow him to assume a unique agency in his antislavery oratory. First, within ostensible presentation of "facts" or testimony, he offers forceful arguments, either explicitly or implicitly, demonstrating that the boundaries between narration and persuasion shift. By so doing, Douglass demonstrates how the discourses of marginalized rhetors challenge narrow conceptions of the public sphere.
>
> Second, highlighting his shifts from narration to persuasion in rhetoric that features his personal experiences, Douglass subtly calls attention to his command of both the "facts" and the "philosophy" of slavery. These strategies allow him to simultaneously negotiate his audiences' preconceptions, challenge the assumptions on which these expectations are based, and create effective antislavery arguments that expand the boundaries of the narrative form.[34]

We see Douglass-like similarities in Taylor's narrative strategies. In fact, Bacon's description of Douglass's shift "from narration to persuasion" is nearly the same as our claim that the art of eloquence functions as persuasion and persuasion as argument. Similar to Douglass's narrative, Taylor's narrative is informed by the art of eloquence, persuasion, and argument.

Thus Taylor's art of eloquence empowers his audiences to hear sacred rhetoric. It is like attending a public reading from a novel or short story or like observing a playwright's plot unfold upon a stage. We find this to be a significant characteristic in Taylor's sacred rhetoric: his peculiar manner. "Literature is communication," Taylor once wrote.[35] While observing Taylor teach homiletics to a class of students, one writer made these observations:

> On one of the days I attend his class, Taylor produces a snatch of paper ripped from the previous Sunday's New York Times Book Review, which he reads religiously, along with the New Republic, The New York Review of Books, and the daily New York Times and News Day. Taylor read the class [a] review listing the ingredients of a great novel—from its descriptive power to its presentation of a wide view of humanity losing its link to individual character. He reminds them that great preaching contains the same elements.[36]

Of import here, Taylor was aware of the rules of composition and rhetoric commonly found in literature and novels and how those same rules can function in a sermon narrative. Where there is composition and rhetoric, literature and novels, there is the art of eloquence. What follows is an example of how literature affects Taylor's sacred rhetoric in "Seeing Our Hurts with God's Eyes." We will notice the shape, form, and movement that are similar to that which is found in a short story:

> But it is that Thursday evening, on the eve of the morrow when the debt will be met in full. It is the last time in the body that our Lord will be with his friends. They will never again see him with the palms unmarked and with the scars not in the feet. The little punctures in the countenance, forever after when they see him, will be there. It is the last time they will see an unbroken Savior. He's talking with them, seeking to rally them against the chills that wait for them and the indignities that will be visited upon them. He tells them many words, among the most tender he ever uttered.[37]

Taylor sets rhetorical boundaries; he describes for his audience the importance of a specific day, "that Thursday evening," and the significance of what follows: "on the eve of the morrow when the debt will be met in full." He employs pathos to point us toward the future, which is postresurrection: "It is the last time in the body that our Lord will be with his friends. They will never again see him with the palms unmarked and with the scars not in the feet. The little punctures in the countenance, forever after when they see him, will be there." These words paint a word picture of Jesus' anatomy, and vividly; forever we will envision the distance traveled between Jesus' hands and his feet. Subtly, Taylor inserts the words "our Lord," an intentional word choice that places us within his rhetorical boundaries and contours of the scene. This is the work of a novelist.

At this our chapter's end, we have demonstrated how Gardner Taylor has mastered the art of eloquence. It is his peculiar manner. His crafted sacred rhetoric transcends theological boundaries and sociopolitical and cultural constructs. His sacred rhetoric is in narrative form. Taylor's art of eloquence shapes his narrative's contours and boundaries as a frame enhances a portrait that is mounted and hangs in an exclusive art gallery. Simply, it is beautiful to hear. His art of eloquence is his signature, and it sets his sacred rhetoric uniquely apart. It is powerful and unforgettable. For this, and for nearly a century, he stands recognized as an eminent pulpiteer.

Epigraph

Edward P. J. Corbett and Robert J. Connors, *Classical Rhetoric for the Modern Student*, 4th ed. (Oxford: Oxford University Press, 1999), 1.

NOTES

1. Joseph Evans, "Vernon Johns and the 'The Romance of Death,'" *American Baptist Quarterly* 25, no. 2 (Summer 2016), 152. Also see "King's Dream: Representation of the Revelation of Democratic Justice," *American Baptist Quarterly* 37 (Spring 2018), 52–67.

2. Michael Eric Dyson, "Gardner Taylor: Poet Laureate of the Pulpit," *Christian Century* (January 4-11, 1995), 14–15. What follows is a portion of Dyson's account of the religion, politics, and death that occurred during a National Baptist Convention USA, Inc., annual session.

Less satisfying was the outcome of the bitter 1960 confrontation between Taylor and J. H. Jackson, then president of the National Baptist Convention, U.S.A., Inc., the nation's third-largest Protestant denomination and the group to which most black Baptists belong. Jackson's conservative social and political views put him at odds with

Martin Luther King, Jr. and those ministers sympathetic to the cause of civil rights and the issue of incumbency (Jackson had been president of the convention since 1953 and in the process broke convention limits on presidential tenure). Taylor agreed to run for the convention presidency at its annual meeting in Kansas in 1960.

A bitter fracas ensued. Hundreds of supporters of each candidate physically struggled and fought, leading to the accidental death of a loyal Jackson supporter and certain defeat for Taylor's team. The next year Taylor joined with King and other ministers who seceded from the National Baptist Convention, Inc., to form the Progressive National Baptist Convention, Inc., which currently has a membership of more than 2 million.

3. Gardner C. Taylor, "Facing Facts with Faith," in *The Words of Gardner Taylor*, comp. Edward L. Taylor, vol. 4: *Special Occasion and Expository Sermons* (Valley Forge, PA: Judson Press, 2001), 114–19.

4. Richard Lischer, ed., *The Company of Preachers: Wisdom on Preaching, Augustine to Present* (Grand Rapids, MI: Eerdmans, 2002), 104.

5. Lane Cooper, ed., *The Rhetoric of Aristotle* (Englewood Cliffs, NJ: Prentice Hall, 1932), xx. Cooper comments on Aristotle's claim that rhetoric is persuasive:

> The merit of the treatise [rhetoric as persuasion] may be stated thus. It is a searching study of the audience, or, to use Aristotle's frequent term, of the "judge," the person (or person) to whom your speech is directed. A speech is to be judged by its effect upon someone. . . . The speaker or writer must know the nature of the soul he wishes to persuade. That is, he must know human nature, with is ways of reasoning, its habits, desires, and emotions, and must know the kind of argument that will persuade each kind of men, as also the emotional appeal that will gain their assent; every detail, the choices of the individual words and phrases, the arrangement of larger and smaller parts, each single item in the speech is to be determined by its effect upon the soul. Since everyone is alternatively listener and speaker, or reader and writer, the Rhetoric thus becomes a popular treatise on the interest of men in groups of individuals, as popular logic, and a popular account of the emotions, the memory, the imagination in hope and fear, and the will.

See Corbett and Connors, *Classical Rhetoric for the Modern Student*, 1: "Rhetoric is the art or the discipline that deals with the use of discourse, either spoken or written, to inform or persuade or motivate an audience, whether that audience is made up of one person or a group of persons."

6. Jonathan S. Kahn, *Divine Discontent: The Religious Imagination of W. E. B. Du Bois* (Oxford: Oxford University Press, 2009), 12. Kahn makes all students of rhetoric take notice. In this instance, we notice that rhetoric without a moral attachment and full conviction of religious faith can be dangerous and used as a form of demagoguery. Kahn characterizes Du Bois closely as using religious language only to attach other priorities that he believes are necessary to address in a way that people of African descent in the United States and ultimately globally can hear his claims. Kahn, however, does concede that Du Bois was authentically religious in a broad sense. What Kahn means is that Du Bois was a religious pragmatic. He does concede furthermore that Du Bois was complicated in the sense that his use of biblical language might mean that he was skeptical of institutional religion and narrowly Christianity that was and is informed by Eurocentrism. Du Bois must be considered a liberal Protestant Christian focused on the humanity of Jesus of Nazareth. The following lengthy excerpt is included here to understand Kahn's claim that an individual can appropriate religious language, a common language to the masses, as a way to underline otherness:

> Religious vocabularies enable Du Bois to craft ends that appear to sit in tension with one another. On the one hand, Du Bois uses religious modalities to argue for black people as a fundamental, irreplaceable part of the larger American nation; in this there is integrationist force to his use of religious vocabulary. On the other hand, Du Bois uses religion to fashion a sense of black peoplehood central to his conception of black American identity. Religion enables Du Bois to bind black people—through hope, love, and at times reprimand. In other words, religious modalities allow him to chart a taut and dialectical path between a unifying account of American democracy that includes black and white together and an account of black identity with an integrity of its own, Du Bois' version of a "nation within a nation."

7. Gardner C. Taylor, "Seeing Our Hurts with God's Eyes," in *The Words of Gardner Taylor*, comp. Edward L. Taylor, vol. 2: *Sermons from the Middle Years, 1970–1980* (Valley Forge, PA, 2000), 87.

8. Martha Simmons and Brad Braxton, "What Happened to Sacred Eloquence? (Celebrating the Ministry of Gardner C. Taylor)," in *Our Sufficiency Is of God: Essays on Preaching in Honor of Gardner C. Taylor*, ed.

Timothy George, James Earl Massey, and Robert Smith Jr. (Macon, GA: Mercer University Press, 2010), 272–73. Simmons and Braxton make a significant contribution to our understanding of eloquence. They point out that Taylor's eloquence was in his "voice." We agree and will make efforts to expand our meaning of eloquence to include style. Style is more than vocal performance and quality. Style belongs to perspicuity, which is purity, precision, propriety: purity of words, precision of words, and propriety of words. Eloquence intersects with all other elements of rhetoric, however; here eloquence intersects with the syntactical arrangement and organization of words, phrases, sentences, and paragraphs.

9. Cooper, *Rhetoric of Aristotle*, 9.

10. Lischer, *Company of Preachers*, 104.

11. Edward L. Taylor, "Gardner C. Taylor: America's Twentieth-Century Preacher," in *The Words of Gardner Taylor*. Taylor's introduction appears in all six volumes of Gardner Taylor's works that were published by Judson Press.

12. See Jacqueline Bacon, *The Humblest May Stand Forth: Rhetoric, Empowerment, and Abolition* (Columbia: University of South Carolina Press, 2002), 60–63.

13. Ibid., 20.

14. Garry Wills, *Lincoln at Gettysburg: The Words That Remade America* (New York: Simon & Schuster, 1992), 263. Wills points out that the following is Lincoln's final text:

> Four score and seven years ago our fathers brought forth on this continent, a new nation, conceived in Liberty, and dedicated to the proposition that all men are created equal.
>
> Now we are engaged in a great civil war, testing whether that nation, or any nation so conceived and so dedicated, can long endure. We are met on a great battle-field of that war. We have come to dedicate a portion of that field, as a final resting place for those who here gave their lives that that nation might live. It is altogether fitting and proper that we should do this.
>
> But, in a larger sense, we cannot dedicate—we cannot consecrate—we cannot hallow—this ground. The brave men, living and dead, who struggled here, have consecrated it, far above our poor power to add or detract. The world will little note, nor long remember what we say here, but it can never forget what they did here. It is for us the living, rather, to be dedicated here to the unfinished work which they who

fought here have thus far so nobly advanced. It is rather for us to be here dedicated to the great task remaining before us—that from these honored dead we take increased devotion to that cause for which they gave the last full measure of devotion—that we here highly resolve that these dead shall not have died in vain—that this nation, under God, shall have a new birth of freedom—and that government of the people, by the people, for the people, shall not perish from the earth.

15. Ibid.

16. Harper Lee, *To Kill a Mockingbird* (New York: HarperPerennial Modern Classics, 2002), 231–34. Note that eloquence, persuasion, and argument intersect. In this way, Lee's narrative persuades. In order to provide an example of how ethos, logos, and pathos are used in a narrative, included here are parts of Atticus Finch's closing argument:

> The state has not produced one iota of medical evidence to the effect that the crime Tom Robinson is charged with ever took place. It has relied instead upon the testimony of two witnesses whose evidence has not only been called into serious question on cross-examination, but has been flatly contradicted by the defendant. The defendant is not guilty, but somebody in this courtroom is. . . .
>
> And so a quiet, respectable, humble Negro who had the unmitigated temerity to "feel sorry" for a white woman has had to put his word against two white people's. I need not remind you of their appearance and conduct on the stand—you saw them for yourselves. The witnesses for the state, with the exception of the sheriff of Maycomb County, have presented themselves to you gentlemen, to this court, in the cynical confidence that their testimony would not be doubted, confident that you gentlemen would go along with them on the assumption—the evil assumption—that *all* Negroes lie, that *all* Negroes are basically immoral beings, that *all* Negro men are not to be trusted around our women, an assumption one associates with minds of their caliber.
>
> Which, gentlemen, we know is in itself a lie as black as Tom Robinson's skin, a lie I do not have to point out to you. You know the truth, and the truth is this: some Negroes lie, some Negroes are immoral, some Negro men are not to be trusted around women— black or white. But this is a truth that applies to the human race and to no particular race of men. There is not a person in this courtroom

who has never told a lie, who has never done an immoral thing, and there is no man living who has never looked upon a woman without desire. . . .

I'm no idealist to believe firmly in the integrity of our courts and in the jury system—that is not ideal to me, it is a living, working reality. Gentlemen, a court is no better than each man of you sitting before me on this jury. A court is only as sound as its jury, and a jury is only as sound as the men who make it up. I am confident that you gentlemen will review without passion the evidence you have heard, come to a decision, and restore this defendant to his family. In the name of God, do your duty.

17. Cooper, *Rhetoric of Aristotle*, 8–9.

18. Ibid., 8.

19. Taylor, "Seeing Our Hurts with God's Eyes," 86–87.

20. Cooper, *Rhetoric of Aristotle*, 9.

21. We obtained a copy of Taylor's official transcript from Oberlin College. Taylor entered the institution in 1937 and officially graduated in 1940.

22. Richard Lischer, *The Preacher King: Martin Luther King Jr. and the Word That Moved America* (Oxford: Oxford University Press, 1995), 41.

23. Ibid., 64–65. Lischer writes:

At the same time that King was learning the vocabulary of liberalism at Crozer [now Colgate Rochester Crozer Divinity School], he was receiving this first classroom instruction in homiletics. He took a whopping nine courses in homiletics, most of them with Robert Keighton, a journeyman instructor who, judged by his later comments, does not appear to have appreciated the gifts and potential of his talented pupil. Keighton's approach to preaching was heavy with nineteenth-century poetry, saturated with sentiment, and driven by the liberal agenda from preaching articulated by Henry Ward Beecher fifty years earlier: that "of moving men from a lower to a higher life . . . inspiring them toward a nobler manhood." On King's handwritten bibliography for his homiletics course, he placed a star beside Halford Luccock's popular In the Minister's Workshop. The aim of many of the texts, including Luccock's, was to locate preaching within a larger and nobler cultural enterprise.

The manuals of the 1930's and 40's were saturated with quotations from the cream of the nineteenth-century Western [Scottish] belles lettres and seasoned with anecdotes from the lives of heroic Scottish preachers. The texts make for embarrassing reading today . . . because in their tone of high-minded nobility they are oblivious to the social ferment and material misery that existed at the time of their writing.

24. Fredrick Douglass, *Narrative of the Life of Frederick Douglass, an American Slave*, introduction and notes by Robert G. O'Meally (New York: Barnes and Noble Classics, 2003), 45.

25. D. H. Dilbeck, *Frederick Douglass: America's Prophet* (Chapel Hill: University of North Carolina Press, 2018), 85.

26. Caleb Bingham, "Dialogue between a Master and Slave," in *The Columbian Orator: Containing a Variety of Original and Selected Pieces Together with Rules, Which Are Calculated to Improve Youth and Others, in the Ornament and Useful Art of Eloquence*, ed. David W. Blight (New York: New York University Press, 1998), 211.

27. Olivia B. Waxman, "'What to the Slave Is the Fourth of July?' The History of Frederick Douglass' Searing Independence Day Oration," *Time*, July 5, 2019, https://time.com/5614930/frederick-douglass-fourth-of-july/.

What follows is an excerpt from James A. Calaioaco, *Frederick Douglass and the Fourth of July* (Kindle edition):

Douglass's audience at Corinthian Hall expected a long speech. His speeches averaged two hours in length, and his July Fourth oration totals thirty printed pages . . . Douglass often spoke extemporaneously, enabling him to adjust his speeches to the reactions of an audience. When the occasion allowed, he relied upon his excellent memory, delivering his speeches without notes . . . A substantial and important speech such as the July Fourth oration was written and rehearsed and delivered from manuscript. Douglass probably read parts to his audience, reciting some of its more powerful sections from memory. His style was typical of the nineteenth century, the great age of American oratory, when the public was accustomed to hearing speeches lasting from one to four hours . . . the best speakers were great performers.

See https://www.amazon.com/Frederick-Douglass-Fourth-James-Colaiaco -ebook/dp.

28. Dyson, "Gardner Taylor," 13.

29. Ibid.

30. Gardner C. Taylor, "Introduction," in *The Words of Gardner Taylor*, comp. Edward L. Taylor, vol. 5: *Lectures and Interviews* (Valley Forge, PA: Judson Press, 2001).

31. Jeffrey C. Stewart, *The New Negro: The Life of Alain Locke* (Oxford: Oxford University Press, 2018), 17–18.

32. Ibid., 16.

33. See Edward L. Taylor, "Gardner C. Taylor," 3.

34. Bacon, *The Humblest May Stand Forth*, 61.

35. Gardner C. Taylor, "The Foolishness of Preaching," in *The Words of Gardner Taylor*, comp. Edward L. Taylor, vol. 5: *Lectures and Interviews* (Valley Forge, PA: Judson Press, 2001), 160.

36. Dyson, "Gardner Taylor," 15.

37. Taylor, "Seeing Our Hurts with God's Eyes," 87.

2

The Most Eloquent Man

*For the best definition which, I think, can be given of eloquence is the
Art of speaking in such a manner as to attain the end for which we speak.
Whenever a man speaks or writes, he is supposed, as a rational being, to
have some end in view; either to inform, or to amuse, or to persuade, or,
in some way or other, to act upon his fellow-creatures. He who speaks, or
writes, in such a manner as to adapt all his words most effectually to that
end, is the most eloquent man. —Hugh Blair*

We make an appeal to our fair-minded and enlightened readers. Our appeal is to your reason and emotions and asks
that you consider carefully our claims. Our chief claim is that Gardner Taylor is the personification and representation of Hugh Blair's
"the most eloquent man." Clarence Newsome, a former dean of the
Howard Divinity School, once said that Taylor "stands in a category
unto himself and sets the modern standard for poetic homiletical
eloquence."[1] James Costen, a former president of the Interdenominational Theological Center, said Taylor "stands alone as the president,
dean, provost and master artisan of Black preaching . . . Hearing him
preach gives one the impression that he has a direct pipeline to God.
If I could only hear one sermon, it would be a Taylor sermon."[2]

To that end, and throughout this book, we offer this as a persuasive
and convincing argument. An argument is judged on its content and
eloquence. Eloquence then is possessed by what Blair has described as
the most eloquent man. An eloquent person is a speaker in possession

of the five elements (we use the word *elements* interchangeably with arts and traditions) of rhetoric: invention, discovery (arrangement, discussed within chapter 3), eloquence (style), memory, and delivery.[3] In short, a person who possesses these arts indeed is the most eloquent man. In this light, we have offered this as a thesis: Taylor is among the few pulpit orators who possessed the five elements of rhetoric. The art of eloquence, however, is used the most frequently in the Taylor canon of sermons. In our view, it is rare that this claim can be made about any single orator or preacher. Although Taylor applied himself to mastering the craft of pulpit oratory, he was endowed naturally with these arts of rhetoric which Blair describes as eloquence.

What is even rarer, Taylor's eloquence intersects with the other traditions of rhetoric in nearly every instance that we have discovered. For this reason and others, we suggest strongly that what Taylor achieves through his pulpit oratory is familiar and approximate to that which is located in nineteenth-century Scottish belles lettres rhetoric. Therefore, it is unnecessary to give deliberate attention to other rhetorical traditions because those traditions are beyond our scope. Indeed, we do not attempt to address classical rhetoric as proof that Taylor was a possessor of that tradition. Neither do we find that these traditions reflect or directly complement our claim of Taylor's mastery of eloquence.

Eloquence then is our primary focus as it relates to the Taylor canon and how we understand that Taylor's eloquence is very similar to that which is an immediate function of Scottish belles lettres rhetoric. What is important is that we have discovered a valuable point of departure: for preachers and orators to use Taylor's approach as a model. *We assert that eloquence, with disciplined study and deliberate effort, can be learned, developed, and deployed.* Eloquence is the underlying art that Taylor used to support his oratorical power in the pulpit. The content of this book makes an effort to reinforce this claim.

The Scottish Enlightenment and the Rise of Belles Lettres Rhetoric

All readers will appreciate Taylor's persuasive power, and most will agree that his pulpit oratorical power was grounded in eloquence. We also make a broader claim: there is a traceable line between Taylor's eloquence and Scottish belles lettres rhetoric. It is certain there is an obvious line between some significant abolitionist orators and others in the progressive traditions and sociomarginalized rhetors' and preachers' oratory. We identify the latter with the civil rights era. These lines provide for us the certainty that eloquence, when properly deployed, is an agent of persuasion and convincing.

In the case of African American orators' and preachers' use of Scottish belles lettres, modifications were made. An argument is made here that the nineteenth-century African American orators and preachers understood the rudimentary rules that were taught by eighteenth- and nineteenth-century teachers of the Scottish belles lettres tradition. The African American form, however, was reinvented intentionally.[4] From this new invention, eloquence was deployed as a penetrating weapon, one that results in achieving literacy and liberty that demonstrate what we refer to as psychological liberation.

As mentioned, Scottish belles lettres can be connected to certain African American rhetorical and literary traditions. We have narrowed our interest, however, to African American oratory. This species of oratory we have traced to the eighteenth- and nineteenth-century Scottish Enlightenment. The Enlightenment was a catalyst that reset the role and functions of rhetoric and distanced it from classical rhetoric. In addition, Scottish Enlightenment rhetoric, or belles lettres, led to a reinvention that we refer to as African American belles lettres. Ironically, we assert, the African American Enlightenment began with an adaptation of belles lettres.

The Scottish Enlightenment influenced most of Europe. It became an intellectual tour de force. In part, this happened because advocates of the Enlightenment embraced rationalism and scientific facts and expected reasonable answers to their complex questions. This scientific community biased itself against classical rhetoric because rhetoric was informed in large part by what is called faculty psychology. We offer the following excerpt to provide a more precise meaning to the term:

> The product of faculty psychology, this approach to *pathos* [emotions] depends on the essential commonality of our psychological apparatus. Kames asserts, "The natural signs of emotions, voluntary and involuntary, being nearly the same in all men, form an universal language,

which no distance in tribe, no diversity of tongue, can darken or render doubtful.[5]

That is, all of humanity shares universally common emotions. Therefore, faculty psychology is the study of human nature. Enlightenment thinkers accepted faculty psychology as universal but believed that emotions can be interpreted solely as a subjective aspect of human nature. The paradigm shift that took place during the Enlightenment was an intellectual shift from subjective reasoning to objective reasoning. This is at the center of the idea of the Enlightenment:

> The idea of "the Enlightenment"—what, where, how and who it was, and what it meant—remains a contested one among scholars. But by the turn of the eighteenth century it was becoming clear across Europe that a rapid evolution in thought was under way. In part this was the result of scientific advance: the dethroning of the Ptolemaic view of the universe . . . in favour of the heliocentric view of Copernicus and his followers; the astonishing discoveries of Newton; major mathematical developments by Descartes in geometry, and Leibniz and Newton with the calculus; the invention of the telescope and microscope, and the new natural philosophy of Galileo, Boyle and Hooke. But these achievements in turn betokened a much wider intellectual, social and cultural realignment, away from religion, deference to institutions and received wisdom and towards individual reason, scepticism, and the exchange of ideas. In due course they led to calls for religious toleration, legal rights and moral equality that many princes and governments across Europe found profoundly threatening.[6]

The Enlightenment idea was at the taproot of rapid evolution. There were massive scientific assertions and discoveries that gave more credibility to facts that rivaled traditional understandings of religious faith. This affected rhetoric, which informs the narratives of politics, law, theology, and the ecclesial church, to name some. Rhetoric took broader forms in the Enlightenment period.

As a result, rhetoric in the eighteenth and nineteenth centuries took on new and innovative forms: the Ciceronian, elocution, philosophical, speculative, and belles lettres. The first, the Ciceronian tradition, was taught to children in order for them to learn the basic rules of rhetoric in order to improve these pupils' English grammar.

By grammar is meant compositional arrangement (words, sentences, and paragraphs). This form was generally taught in elementary and primary schools in England and Scotland. The Ciceronian tradition continued to have significant influence during the time of the Scottish Enlightenment era.

A second approach was the elocution movement, or speaking out. "Elocution was adapted as a term for delivery or reading aloud."[7] This included learning voice control and gestures. "Interest in it began to revive with the effort to achieve high standards of delivery in preaching and in theater in the seventeenth century."[8]

A third form of rhetoric in the neoclassical era was philosophical rhetoric. It was based on new logic and perhaps scientific psychology. In some ways, rhetoric which uses syllogisms and enthymemes (deductive and inductive examples and reasoning) was attractive to science. This form of rhetoric seemed to possess what we will generally call rationalism, which was a part of the motivation of the Enlightenment. This form of rhetoric was thought to be useful as a primary way of "improvement of eloquence in English, and especially in rational species of preaching."[9]

A fourth form, similar to the philosophical form, we characterize in general as a kind of speculative rhetoric. By this we mean that its proponents saw rhetoric as a valuable tool to explain philosophical and psychological existential and epistemological dimensions. In short, this refers to a person's knowledge, which is a capacity that comes partly from experience and partly from reflection upon such experiences. This, some believed, was at the taproot of language formation and by extension rhetoric. Scottish Enlightenment leaders such as Lord Kames, Joseph Priestley, and a university professor in Aberdeen, George Campbell, made efforts to understand the nexus between theory, experience, faith, and truth. This may be considered as a modern birth of understanding religious truth claims as subjective in nature.[10]

The fifth form of rhetoric that made its presence known during the Enlightenment was belles lettres. What follows is an excerpt that objectively explains the impact that belles lettres had on the Enlightenment period:

In 1958, two sets of student notes of lectures by Adam Smith on rhetoric and belle lettres were discovered in a library in Scotland. Smith, later to become famous for his pioneering work on capitalism, The Wealth of Nations (1776), had delivered the lectures while teaching moral philosophy at the University of Glasgow in 1762–63, probably elaborating on lectures he had given in Edinburgh earlier. Smith's lectures are the earliest known statement in English of belletristic rhetoric . . . The lectures were not published until 1963, but they exerted an influence on those who had heard them, including Hugh Blair, who later lectured on the same subject in Edinburgh.[11]

Smith focused on the nature and history of language. Beauty is more recognizable when it is dressed in style and neatly presented to an audience, whether it is spoken or written:

Although it was one of Smith's announced objectives to prepare students for activity in public address, he concentrates on giving them an understanding of great classical oratory, especially works of Demosthenes and Cicero, and does not provide a systematic discussion of invention or arrangement. The manuscripts break off at this point. Smith may have continued with observations about British oratory of the recent past.[12]

What is noteworthy, belles lettres is rhetoric of amalgamation. We will firmly attach this characterization of rhetoric to William G. Allen, who was the first known African American professor of belles lettres. Allen thought that belles lettres was an appropriation of the aforementioned forms of rhetoric that emerged during the Scottish Enlightenment period. For Allen, belles lettres rhetoric shapes an argument which is not only persuasive but indeed is convincing. Belles lettres rhetoric then is eloquence. We should think of it as a catalytic agent that persuades and convinces persons to take action. When considered in this way, although eloquence is dressed in neat and appropriate language and its sentences are underlined with beautiful symmetry and balance, its end is to invoke persuasive action.

In short, Scottish belles lettres appropriates all of the Enlightenment's claims. Blair adapted the Enlightenment claims of the superiority of science to help orators to ascertain their objectives. We assert that there was no more of a committed ambassador of the Scottish belles lettres tradition as a new rhetoric than Hugh Blair. These examples are significant to our discussion and help us to place Scottish belles lettres into a proper context. What is more, we highlight that the Scottish Enlightenment had a direct impact upon Blair. The Enlightenment influenced and shaped Blair's worldview, but Blair influenced and shaped the Scottish Enlightenment worldview.

Scottish Belles Lettres Rhetoric and Its Influence on Pulpit Oratory

In order to make our claim further, we inform our readers that in addition to Hugh Blair's prominence as a professor of Scottish belles lettres and a leading proponent of Scottish Enlightenment ideas, he was a Presbyterian preacher. These aspects of Blair, we suggest, underline his beliefs, values, and orientation toward rhetoric and its influence on pulpit eloquence. In this way, we consider that Blair was able to adapt other forms of rhetoric into his Scottish belles lettres, resulting in a kind of amalgamation that we attached earlier to William G. Allen.

Whatever the case, these forms of rhetoric were birthed during the age of the Scottish Enlightenment. In a real sense, Blair created a synthesis between the scientific, fact-based Enlightenment and an appreciation of biblical and secular literature and other social sciences. Blair was able to achieve this because he saw a connection between the Enlightenment and eloquence. Blair and his peers (Smith, Kames, Campbell, Richard Whatley, and others) were capable of understanding the cultural paradigm shift that took place. Like Blair, his peers were prominent thought leaders who helped shape the new cultural worldview. Blair understood that eloquence was agile and could fulfill multiple purposes. Eloquence then is an art that can be used by sacred and secular thinkers to persuade and convince people to take action.

Thus, Blair has provided a timeless definition for eloquence. We now bring to readers' attention the opening epigraph. Blair did not overtly use the word *rhetoric* or clearly express that the most eloquent man is a possessor of the five traditions of rhetoric. Instead, Blair substituted the word *eloquence* as his preferred descriptor. What is more, in the manner that Blair defined eloquence, we apply

and connect it now to our characterization of a species of sociomarginalized people's oratory.

There is a correlation between African American oratory and
that of the eighteenth- and nineteenth-century Scottish church and
university elite of Blair's day. This parallels the Harlem Renaissance
writers, the civil rights era leaders, the Black Power movement, and
more recently, the Black Lives Matter movement. Each movement
was dependent on the masses to demonstrate, but these movements
are led often by university-educated people who could be considered
among the religious and university elite. What is germane here is
that we have made an attempt to demonstrate and underscore what
informed and shaped Blair's understanding of eloquence.

Therefore, we reinforce our assertion that eloquence is a significant
feature that we associate with Blair's version of Scottish belles lettres.
We have highlighted that this is consistent with the eighteenth- and
nineteenth-century emphasis on eloquence in the new rhetoric. When
we consider, however, a more contemporary historical context, new
rhetoric is not so new. Today we clearly would define new rhetoric as
neoclassical rhetoric:

> The most definitive statement of neoclassical rhetoric . . . came from
> Hugh Blair (1718–1800). Blair, like [David] Hume, Smith, and Camp-
> bell, was a part of the Scottish Enlightenment, a group of intellectuals
> who brought a note of dispassionate common sense and reason to phi-
> losophy and literature in the eighteenth century and a note of liberal
> imagination to the dour Calvinism of the North.[13]

Indeed, Blair possessed a liberal imagination that provided rhetorical
space and intellectual distance from Calvinistic dogmatism. During
this period, Blair began to shape the form of his rhetoric into a different hybrid of classical rhetoric. It did retain some of the original
claims of classical rhetoric. Nevertheless, Blair thought it necessary
to rethink the art of rhetoric, seeing an obvious intersection between
eloquence (rhetoric) and other Enlightenment social sciences such as
philosophy and literature. What is of import, Blair was squarely at
the center of the Scottish Enlightenment.

Blair, the author of *Lectures on Rhetoric and Belles Lettres*, used
his lectures to critique and improve upon the value of rhetoric to

those who would stand and make arguments in order to influence persuasively people into action. To do so, Blair sought to broaden rhetoric's pedagogy (methods of teaching). We consider Blair was successful in his efforts, namely, to advance the aim of rhetoric, which is persuasion and conviction. Blair considers persuasion without convincing to be incomplete and thus not reaching its objective, which is human action. That is, the intended outcome is that readers or listeners are more than persuaded but are under conviction. It is conviction that leads to action.

As an example, Paul of Tarsus made a historical testimony of his Christian conversion and its related events. He made an attempt to persuade King Agrippa not only to accept his testimony (his rhetorical argument) but also to follow Jesus of Nazareth (to be persuaded to act). Agrippa appreciated Paul's rhetoric but was not convinced: "'Are you going to persuade me to become a Christian so easily?' 'I wish before God,' replied Paul, 'that whether easily or with difficulty, not only you but all who listen to me today might become as I am—except for these chains'" (Acts 26:28b-29).[14]

Neoclassical rhetoric, or new rhetoric, then is centered on achieving conviction with support of ethical and emotional pleas upon human nature. This is at the taproot of our claim that Gardner Taylor is the most eloquent man:

> To be an eloquent speaker, in the proper sense of the word, is far from being either a common or an easy attainment. Indeed, to compose a florid harangue on some popular topic, and to deliver it so as to amuse an audience, is a matter not very difficult. But though some praise be due to this, yet the idea which I have endeavoured to give of eloquence, is much higher. It is a great exertion of the human powers. It is the art of being persuasive and commanding: the art not of pleasing the fancy merely; but of speaking both to the understanding and to the heart; of interesting the hearers in such a degree, as to seize and carry them along with us; and to leave them with a deep and strong impression of what they have heard. How many talents, natural and acquired, must concur for carrying this to perfection? A strong, lively, and warm imagination; quick sensibility of heart, joined with solid judgment, good sense, and presence of mind; all improved by great and long attention to style and composition; and supported also by

the exterior, yet important qualifications, of a graceful manner, a presence not ungainly, and a full and tuneable voice. How little reason to wonder, that a perfect and accomplished orator should be one of the characters that is most rarely to be found! Let us not despair, however. Between mediocrity and perfection, there is a wide interval.[15]

Eloquence, as Blair expresses it, has similar goals that are shared with marginalized orators. It serves as a model for a species of African American orators and preachers. What began in the eighteenth and nineteenth centuries continued into the twentieth century, and in some very limited spaces continues into the twenty-first century. Our focus, however, is primarily limited to eloquence and its influence upon the pulpit oratory of the twentieth century and the early decades of the twenty-first-century pulpit icon Gardner Taylor, the most eloquent man.

Eloquence and Social Justice

The connection between Scottish belles lettres and a sociomarginalized hybrid is evident when we consider the significance of literacy and liberty, which is an oppressed people's constant and dogged pursuit. To its end, what emerges is justice motifs. This is reinforced by Glen McClish's thorough treatment of William G. Allen's prodigious work. McClish has distinguished himself as a noteworthy scholar of African American rhetoric. Here he is interested in Allen's rhetoric and rhetorical strategy. Allen was the first African American university professor of belles lettres.

> It is most fitting, then, as a rhetor, Allen employed a kind of intentional amalgamation, drawing on all available means of persuasion and the traditions of oratory to further social justice . . . Advocating neither an obsequious imitation nor outright rejection of the rhetorical practices and traditions of the white power structure, Allen strives pragmatically to overturn America's pervasive [nineteenth-century] racism and usher in an era of true freedom.[16]

It is clear that Allen's amalgamation is another description of Blair's inclusion of the Scottish Enlightenment's social sciences that

Blair employed to inform his version of eloquence. An eloquent orator demonstrates that she or he is free to think. Indeed, such an orator is more than a "pompous flatterer":

> It is an observation made by several writers, that eloquence is to be looked for only in free states. Longinus, in particular, at the end of his treatise on the sublime, when assigning the reason why so little sublimity of genius appeared in the age wherein he lived, illustrates this observation with a great deal of beauty. Liberty, he remarks, is the nurse of true genius; it animates the spirit, and invigorates the hopes of men; excites honourable emulation, and a desire of excelling in every art. All other qualifications, he says, you may find among those who are deprived of liberty; but never did a slave become an orator; he can only be a pompous flatterer.[17]

Of course, Blair did not grasp the humanity of the unyielding bondsmen and other sociomarginalized people, and neither had he heard or met Allen. In the following excerpt, Jacqueline Bacon provides perhaps the most insightful portrait of Allen and his understanding of how eloquence functions. Let us add that Bacon provides readers a stark contrast between Blair's and Allen's views over what forms the ability and capacity to learn and develop eloquence:

> In 1852, William G. Allen, one of the three African American professors at New York Central College in McGrawville, spoke to the institution's Dialexian Society on orators and oratory. His speech articulates the converse, in effect, of Frederick Douglass's comments about silence and slavery. "Orations worthy the name must have for their subject political liberty," Allen maintains, "and orators worthy of the name must necessarily originate in the nation that is on the eve of passing from a state of slavery into freedom, or from a state of freedom into slavery. How could this be otherwise? Where there is no pressure, the highest efforts of genius must lie undeveloped." Significantly, Allen more explicitly connects the experience of oppression to powerful rhetoric: "I was about to say, that orators worthy the name, must originate among the oppressed races, but on turning to the pages of history, I was reminded of the fact, that all races, with scarcely an exception, had, at some period of their existence, been in a state of thraldom." The most powerful oratory, then, arises from oppression,

and rhetoric is fundamentally connected to the transition from slavery to freedom. If, as Douglass maintains, "there comes no *voice* from the enslaved," it is also true that it is an act of freedom and resistance to oppression to speak for oneself, to determine one's own discourse. If silence and slavery are linked, so are freedom and rhetoric.[18]

Oratory or eloquence, for Allen, is predominately heard and located in the margins of the oppressed. Where there is a yearning for freedom, it requires political liberty or political genius and courageous action. It is pressure upon the oppressed that creates rhetorical genius. We would rephrase that: it is "oppression" that creates rhetorical genius. The notion that persons who are not free are nothing more than a pompous flatterer, however, would have been understood by nineteenth-century sociomarginalized orators and preachers.

This is understood no less in the twentieth and twenty-first centuries by the oppressed. Throughout this book, we attach Allen's understanding of eloquence to that of Taylor. Nevertheless, like Blair, Allen employed all available traditions to persuade and convince against racism and white power structures in order to pursue true freedom. In addition, we too firmly attach this example to our original claim. There is an apparent connection between Blair's brand of Scottish belles lettres and Allen's brand of African American belles lettres. The connection is a thirst for penetrating rhetoric that ends in psychological liberation. This is the freedom of the soul.

Alongside Campbell and Whatley, Blair was considered a part of "the great triumvirate" of Scottish rhetoricians. They were influential scholars of the revival of rhetoric that began in fifth-century Greece.[19] There is much that could be written about classical rhetoric, but as previously mentioned, we have chosen to narrow our scope to that which is germane to our interest.

We add here our preferred definition of eloquence that was pointed toward Frederick Douglass, but it is tasteful to expand this definition to include Taylor's pulpit oratory:

Socrates used to say that all men are sufficiently eloquent in that which they understand. Cicero says that, though this is plausible, it is not strictly true. He adds that no man can be eloquent even if he understands the subject ever so well but is ignorant how to form and to polish his speech. We take these views for what they are worth, but venture to add that eloquence is a spontaneous outburst of the human soul.[20]

Readers will see later that eloquence is attractive and how it is attached to Taylor. For now, we continue with the contributions of Blair to Scottish belles lettres.

As was previously mentioned, during Blair's professional life, many professors of rhetorical studies were aligned closely with university appointments, which resulted in an intellectual revival of rhetoric—the new rhetoric. Placed in its historical context, the revival appeared during the so-called university movement (once again Blair's university movement parallels the Harlem Renaissance, the civil rights era, and the Black Power and Black Lives Matter movements). The movement was influenced by the Scottish Enlightenment and elocution. Of concern to us, throughout Blair's writings the descriptor "rhetoric" is rarely used in his lectures on the discipline of persuasion.

In addition to Blair being an ordained Presbyterian minister and the Regius Professor of Rhetoric and Belles Lettres at the University of Edinburgh, he was a native of Edinburgh and a graduate of the University of Edinburgh. Also Blair served as pastor of the Canongate Church and then St. Giles Church until his retirement. While at Canongate Church, Blair became the successor to the widely popular and influential rhetorician and philosopher Adam Smith, the author of *The Wealth of Nations*. Smith's work continues to have influence on Eurocentrism, and perhaps the book is as much about human nature as it is about economics.

One writer explains: "I have come to understand that *Wealth of Nations* was underpinned by his *Theory of Moral Sentiments*," which was one of Smith's earlier works. Smith in the latter argues that people can have two impulses that function simultaneously. Smith, the writer believes, "anticipated a range of contemporary events . . . One such is the rise of celebrity politics, from the interaction of modern technology with human disposition to admire the rich and powerful, and the human capacity for mutual sympathy."[21] What is of import, we emphasize, is that Scottish thinkers focused on human nature, as did their ancient predecessors in the study of the art of rhetoric.

The art emerged as rhetoricians, philosophers, and others began to observe and study tendencies and habits of human nature. By human nature, we mean how humans behave cognitively. Of course this takes into consideration how people reason and how humans express emotions:

> Reason, eloquence, and every art which ever has been studied among mankind, may be abused, and may prove dangerous in the hands of bad men; but it were perfectly childish to contend, that, upon this account, they ought to be abolished. Give truth and virtue the same arms which you give vice and falsehood, and the former are likely to prevail. Eloquence is no the invention of the schools. Nature teaches every man to be eloquent, when he is much in earnest. Place him in some critical situation; let him have some great interest at stake, and you will see him lay hold of the most effectual means of persuasion. The art of oratory proposes nothing more than to follow out that track which nature has pointed out. And the more exactly that this track is pursued, the more that Eloquence is properly studied, the more shall we be guarded against the abuse which bad men make of it, and enabled the better to distinguish between true eloquence and the tricks of sophistry.[22]

The art of rhetoric then becomes sacred only when it is employed for sacred purposes. There is neither a secular nor a sacred cognitive process employed by an elementary school teacher who is committed to teaching children how to read. Methods may vary, but the goal is the same: that students learn to recognize and pronounce the letters of the alphabet, recognize and pronounce vowel sounds, and recognize the different functions of vowels and consonants. These skills become a function of repetition and so forth. Afterward, children learn to read for comprehension, and this includes an ability to differentiate secular and sacred texts. Social norms and expectations help in this regard. If religious conversion takes hold and influences one's worldview, reading sacred narratives then becomes a sacred act because the reader understands seriously, if not reverently, sacred things. In a similar fashion, there is no difference in learning the rudimentary rules and guidelines that inform the art of rhetoric or, as Blair prefers, eloquence.

Eloquence, Literacy, and Liberty

We now compare and contrast two very different cultures which ironically shared the same eighteenth- and nineteenth-century goals. Our study begins in Scotland. The Scottish people understood that literacy leads to liberty. This was a part of their long-term strategy. That is, the Scottish people built impressive universities and other supportive forms of education. By creating a premier European education, Scotland forced England to address hegemonic practices that protected obvious and deliberate income and wealth inequalities.[23] In short, Scotland sought liberty through literacy, and as a result, Scotland and England were intellectually and economically integrated. Scotland freed itself from England's oppressive tentacles:

> In the 18th century, Scotland had four well-established universities, which were quite different from their English counterparts (Oxford, Cambridge). The terrain and climate of Scotland greatly influenced the development of these universities, which were formed to serve an isolated and poor people who wanted desperately to be educated and who surmounted great odds to secure that goal. The southern universities, particularly Edinburgh, served a large urban population, many of whom attended the university lectures for the pure joy of learning. The 1707 Act of Union, combining the parliaments of Scotland and England, brought about great prosperity because Scotland was no longer excluded from profitable overseas trade by the Navigation Acts or hampered by tariffs in its trade with England.[24]
>
> Over the centuries, the Scots had developed an educational system that was in fact superior to England's in many ways and was admirably suited to their people. Their universities were highly respected on the Continent and in England, and the influence of their graduates in the establishment of universities in the new world has been well documented.[25]

What is germane to our focus, Scotland understood that liberal education prepared its society and citizens to engage in a rhetorical and economic battle to gain its liberty—but that battle required literacy. We cannot overlook that the Scottish people were a part of Eurocentrism and made large contributions to its welfare in Europe and in the birth of America. John Witherspoon, the only clergyperson to sign the American Declaration of Independence, was a Scottish immigrant.

During that time (and recently similar views have reemerged during the Trump era), African Americans were viewed as less than human. Candidly, African American personality and bodies were accepted vaguely as a part of the human family. Blacks on predominately European continents were not a part of the Eurocentric segue of literacy to liberty. In what would become the United States, blacks arrived in 1619, not as immigrants but as slaves. In most instances, blacks were not considered anything more than three-fifths of persons. Still, the nineteenth-century African American intellectuals reinvented Scottish rhetoric for their own purposes, which empowered them to advocate for their universal rights and the abolishment of slavery.

This was due in large part to some gaining access to the power of rhetorical education. Thus, literacy to liberty was the end goal which led leaders to create a universal value of literacy. Though most blacks were slaves, African American freedmen created what can be considered their own universities and supportive school systems, as Jacqueline Bacon and Glen McClish indicate:

> Philadelphia's African-American literary societies seem to have drawn from the tradition of nineteenth-century American university education that was heavily indebted to Scottish faculty psychology of the previous century. Central to this educational framework was highly influential rhetorical pedagogy. As Nan Johnson argues, this tradition of training in eloquence built on fundamental principles set forth by Scots George Campbell, Hugh Blair, Lord Kames, and—indirectly— Adam Smith, including the presupposition that the mind works according to natural and universal laws.[26]

For people of African descent, their literary societies served as their university education. Like the Scots before them, people of African descent relied heavily on learning the persuasive power of eloquence. If Bacon and McClish are correct, African American rhetors and preachers appropriated the dominating culture's rhetoric, which was reinvented for multiple effects. Its most significant effect was faculty psychology. Their goal was to affect the oppressor and the oppressed psyche—that is, moral and ethical use of persuasion and convincing to liberate the oppressed.

Bacon and McClish provide illustrative storylines that dramatize the necessity for people of African descent to pursue freedom in haste. What follows is the story of freedman (woman) Sarah Douglass and the horrors that are associated with being a member of the wretched of the earth:

> One short year ago, how different were my feelings on the subject of slavery! It is true, the wail of the captive sometimes came to my ear in the midst of my happiness, and caused my heart to bleed for his wrongs; but . . . I had formed a little world of my own, and cared not to move beyond its precincts. But how was the scene changed when I beheld the oppressor lurking on the border of my own peaceful home! I saw his iron hand stretched forth to seize me as his prey, and the cause of the slave became my own. I started up . . . and determined, by the help of the Almighty, to use every exertion in my power to elevate the character of my wronged and neglected race.[27]

Douglass was the daughter of abolitionists Robert Douglass and Grace Bustil Douglass. She was an educator and abolitionist and active in Philadelphia's Female Anti-Slavery Society. Douglass used her literary society, which was an example of people of African descent's university system, to give penetrating addresses that inspired others to advocate for the liberation of people of African descent.

We suggest that Douglass's eloquence parallels that of Blair. What is different, however, is that Douglass's eloquence points toward racial uplift. It is clear her horrific experience with her oppressor's lust for power over her black body inspired what some may call self-help rhetoric: "I . . . determined, by the help of the Almighty, to use every exertion in my power to elevate the character of my wronged and neglected race." Bacon adds, "Douglass calls attention to American society's oppression of African Americans and implies that self-help is a form of resistance."[28] Bacon continues, "Douglass's realization of the threats posed to her by a racist white society transcends the abstract realm, suggesting to her audience that self-help does not merely encompass theoretical moral principles but also leads to concrete action for survival."[29]

We point out here that Sarah Douglass, however, needed to be convinced through direct experience that oppression is a threat to the liberty of all people. Indeed, there were many Sarah Douglasses who had quarantined their minds from the ills of society. Richard Lischer points toward this kind of psychological indifference to oppression that frustrated Martin Luther King Jr.:

> In a sermon entitled "Ingratitude," he voices his usual complaint, but with a greater-than-usual bitterness, against the ingratitude of success-ful blacks who quickly forget the sacrifices of others. "I say to you this morning they are ingrates. . . . [They say,] 'Oh, I'm the first Negro here.' And they think it just happened. They talk about the jobs they have and, and, they think it happened out of benevolence of industry."[30]

Although Sarah Douglass was a member of a sociomarginalized community, she was psychologically indifferent to the evil institution of slavery and the degradation that others endured for their entire lives: "I had formed a little world of my own, and cared not to move beyond its precincts." There is no doubt Douglass had blocked psy-chologically the larger implications of what it means to be black in America. In short, Douglass is representative of many women and men in church pews where we will stand and preach. Preachers pro-claim a liberating gospel to people who are indifferent to the pain and suffering endured by others in many places in the world.

It is unfortunate that King knew some twentieth-century Sarah Douglasses. In his time, King had to confront people who had this Douglass-like psychological block. In King's time, there were mid-dle-class blacks who had distanced themselves from fellow blacks who were suffering under Jim Crow and Jane Crow and segrega-tion's hegemonic policies—unethical and immoral policies that were designed to reinforce bigotries, racism, and sexism. In order to preach to the indifferent, there is no doubt that we need amalgamation rhet-oric to inform our pulpit oratory. A pulpit orator must understand the psychological grip that lies at the taproot of our contemporary indifference. It is indifference that possesses people and leaves us spiritually paralyzed, morally powerless, and uncourageously ambiv-alent about human degradation and suffering.

Eloquence and Psychology

Our objective then is to encourage preachers to learn, develop, and deploy eloquence as a persuasive and convincing agent. We add now that psychology has an important role to fulfill in how we choose to characterize Taylor's eloquence. We assert here that when Taylor preaches a biblical text it creates a natural intersection between the text's narratives and pathologies and between the audience's narratives and pathologies. We mean that Taylor understood that there are at least two pathologies and narratives that function in every sermon discourse. There is one that belongs to the text and a second that belongs to an audience. We keep in mind that a narrative then has an underlining pathology.

It is the pathology of the narrative that points toward our cognitive behavior, our emotional quotient, and our capacity to act upon a clarion call to "the ethical." As an example, we point to the eloquence of Jesus of Nazareth: "The Spirit of the Lord is on me, because he has anointed me to preach the good news to the poor. He has sent me to proclaim release to the captives and recovery of sight to the blind, to set free the oppressed, to proclaim the year of the Lord's favor" (Luke 4:18-19).

There is no clearer example of that which we claim. Indeed, Jesus is eloquent. He creates a narrative that doubles between the text and his audience (this is an example of the kind of intersection that we just mentioned). In addition, his eloquence doubles and surfaces as two pathologies. There is a pathology that belongs to those who appear with Jesus in the text. There is a pathology that belongs to those who recognize that their pathology intersects with that of the text.

In this way, Jesus of Nazareth speaks to our faculty psychology. We hear him direct the gospel message toward the poor, the captives, the blind, and the oppressed. His words trigger something within the human psyche; his words invoke challenging advice, which is that we are duty-bound to engage in ethical human behavior. Of course we can claim this is an act of the Spirit; the text plainly states that it is an act of the Holy Spirit. At the same time, we can claim this is a psychological act. In both instances, we understand that human agency begins with an acknowledgment that a narrative persuades and, we add, convinces hearers.

What we refer to as faculty psychology can be understood as mental activity. This provides space for neurological responses in the brain's frontal lobe where these responses originate as linguistic constructs. In the simplest terms possible, this means that when our words are heard by a hearer, spoken words undergo social organization within the brain. The following excerpt seems to reinforce our claim that there is a psychological effect attached to the activity between words and hearers:

> [Mental] activity of the hearer can often be guided by the speaker either by supplying certain arguments bearing on the nature of his own theses or by supplying certain items of information which will encourage his hearers to reason in some particular way. These arguments which take the discourse itself as their object, and these items of information likely to arouse such arguments, can also come from a third party: the speaker's opponent, particularly in legal debate or perhaps from a mere spectator.[31]

Of import are the similarities between our claims, namely, that the speaker's or pulpit orator's narrative bears upon human nature (psyche). The pulpit orator's words are interpreted, translated, and grounded into the hearer's reasonability. Thus, in this instance, the biblical text's narrative and pathology now intersect with the personal and collective narratives and pathologies of the hearer. This is where psychology, rhetoric, and cognition intersect.[32]

We suggest that Taylor either directly or indirectly understood this claim. It is evident in the way that Taylor often proclaims his discourse's narrative with its supporting arguments in an adroit and unassuming fashion. His prose is beautiful and symmetrical. His prose is the personification of eloquence, and it draws audiences into his narrative psychologically. Take notice of how Taylor provides what we will refer to throughout this book as a word picture. What is of interest here is that we follow him and listen carefully to his chosen words as he uses words to create a portrait. This portrait represents human life in a pulpit discourse called "A Cry for Guidance" (Psalm 25:1-2, 4-5):

Life is a road that courses and passes through the years. It starts in the east with the dawn and fresh breezes of youth. How bright the path seems, how confident we are, what a spring and bounce and lilt there are in our steps! How happily we swing our arms and smile as we walk and skip along the road. The road passes through the noonday—how many of us have reached that point! The sun beats steadily upon us and we toil along and time passes quickly. Life is a road. On we go into afternoon . . . "Our shadow begins to fall behind us." Such is a sure sign that the sun that in the morning was at our back is not westering and falling in front of us. On, on into the sunset, the twilight and then the way disappears from human view. We pass out of sight. Life is a journey.[33]

Taylor has painted an eloquent portrait of human life. Notice how Taylor creates life's boundary's edges. They are expressed as a road that courses and passes through the years. Life starts in the eastern skies and ends in the western skies. Life has sunshine and shadows, representing time that passes from morning to twilight when the sun's shadows and neither its light can be perceived by human faculties. Still, life is a road, and life is a journey. This is eloquence. After a protracted introduction, Taylor makes the biblical text plain and visual to his audience. He interweaves quotes from the psalm in his sermon text: "To you, O Lord, I lift up my soul [my psyche]"; "O my God, in you I trust; let me not be put to shame; let not my enemies exult over me"; "Make me to know your ways, O Lord; teach me your paths. Lead me in your truth and teach me, for you are the God of my salvation; for you I wait all the day long!"[34]

We see the images that appear in the portrait. Taylor has painted up and down the canvas. By using words as a paintbrush, Taylor describes the human hopes, dreams, and prayers of every Christian believer. Taylor's eloquence is persuasive and convincing. His narrative is persuasive because it is underlined by a pathology that is shared by the writer of the biblical text and the hearers. This is a psychological act, a mental activity. Taylor reinforces his conclusion in order to convince his hearers to follow Jesus of Nazareth on the path:

We have more to go on than the psalmist. In the long journey of life, Lord, which way shall we turn? The only thing that human wisdom can say to us . . . "I think this is the way you ought to take." "It seems feasible for you to choose this pathway." [Taylor's voice reemerges] On the evidence, wisdom would seem to be on the side of this decision.[35]

Our souls need assurance, some blessed assurance. In the midst of all the world's shrewdness and wisdom there is only one, our Redeemer and our Lord, who says, "I am the way . . . no man cometh to the Father, but by me." Not all your wisdom finds you in the way to life and joy, but Christ is the way. There is no human map to lead you from earth to bright glory, but Christ is the way. We are traveling an uneven journey. Let Jesus lead you. He's a mighty good leader. Happy is the man who can say of our God as we have known him in Christ Jesus.[36]

Besides Taylor's eloquence, we point to his high Christology. He has sought to convince his audience that life is an uneven journey and that it cannot end in satisfaction reliant solely upon the basis of human wisdom. Instead, human wisdom must concede defeat and rest its case, hope, and destiny in the faithful leadership, fellowship, and guidance of Jesus of Nazareth.

As a final note, Taylor demonstrates that words have an invaluable currency and worth which we contend leads human behavior into action.

Action implies assessments of situations and the people with whom the person interacts. It implies reflection upon one's interests, sentiments, purposes, and those of others. Human beings are animals and have biological natures, but they differ from other animals in the range and significance of their use of symbols, of language. They understand their world by depicting it in symbols and by placing meaning on events. . . . As [Kenneth] Burke wrote somewhere, human beings are the only animals who can see signs as signs. Both the dramatist and the sociologist must take cognizance of the difference between motion and action.

[Burke writes:] Stimuli do not possess an absolute meaning. Even a set of signs indicating the likelihood of death by torture has another meaning in the orientation of a comfort-loving skeptic than it would for the ascetic whose world-view promised eternal reward for martyrdom. Any given situation derives its character from the entire framework by which we judge it.[37]

We take seriously that action is assessed differently in dissimilar situations and that people interact differently with other people in a variety of ways. In addition, we find it quite significant that people have a natural ability to understand a range of symbols, and what each symbol means in dissimilar events. And we take note: words are merely symbols that are used to create forms of stimulus for a person or persons who experience these stimuli differently. Because people are informed by their preconditioned worldviews, this is truthful.

The preacher who has studied the psychological effect that is the power of words increases her or his mastery of eloquence. We remember that eloquence is "Speech is a powerful lord that with the smallest and most invisible body accomplishes most godlike works. It can banish fear and remove grief and instill pleasure and enhance pity."[38] Taylor epitomizes this example of eloquence. Although he possessed natural gifts, throughout his pulpit ministry he continued to study eloquence. One of the key aspects of Taylor's eloquence was his working vocabulary, which is another way to describe his mastery of the English language.

In fact, Taylor once described the proper use of language demonstrates command over the biblical text and topic. During a prestigious preaching lecture series, Taylor made the following remarks that seem to reinforce our observation:

> To them [preachers] somehow has been given an alliance, an assembly of gifts, each of which is important to the preaching responsibility but all of which very rarely come together in one person; a clarity of thought, a lucidity of language, a feel for Scripture, the homiletic instinct, a capacity to see in Scripture and out of it the pursuing footprints of God and the hurt that at last takes the shape of the cross. Add to that the fleeing footsteps of our humanity, tragically enough; fleeing from what is our only peace. Add to that the quality of voice which somehow matches the music of language. These cannot be manufactured.[39]

What Taylor describes is similar to Blair's definition of the most eloquent man. Taylor points toward eloquence as a preacher's most prized possession. Eloquence then is a preacher who possesses the five elements of rhetoric. For Taylor, still, it is eloquence that underlines and intersects all available elements.

One can summarize Taylor's comments: a clarity of thought (invention), a feel for Scripture (understanding biblical narrative and its flow), a capacity to see in Scripture (invention, arrangement, and memory), lucidity of language (arrangement, eloquence, and style), homiletic instinct, quality of voice, and music of language (delivery). Taylor demonstrates the psychological power that words have when they are arranged into a grammar. Grammar and the command of language belong to the wordsmith.

Conclusion

In the chapters that follow, we press our thesis: Gardner Taylor is among the few pulpit orators who possessed the five elements of rhetoric (invention, discovery, eloquence and style, memory, and delivery). In order to demonstrate the plausibility of our thesis, we rely upon some of his sermon discourses and homiletic lectures which we have examined from the Taylor canon. What is more, we consider that Taylor's pulpit oratory is an example for how rhetoric functions. In our view, Taylor's pulpit oratory serves as a model for preachers who desire to learn, develop, and deploy the arts of rhetoric in their sermons. Our objective then is to persuade and convince our enlightened readers that this is possible with disciplined study and a commitment to this approach. In order to do so, we make an appeal to your reason and emotions and ask that you consider carefully our claims made throughout this book. Our chief claim is that Gardner Taylor is the personification and representation of Hugh Blair's most eloquent man.

Epigraph

Hugh Blair, "Eloquence or Public Speaking—History of Eloquence—Grecian Eloquence—Demosthenes," in *Lectures on Rhetoric and Belles Lettres*, ed. Linda Ferreira-Buckley and S. Michael Halloran, Landmarks in Rhetoric and Public Address (1783; Carbondale: Southern Illinois University Press, 2005), 264.

NOTES

1. See Raliegh Jones Jr., "Fifteen Greatest Black Preachers Revisited," August 22, 2007, Black Preaching Network, http://abcpreachers.ning.com/forum/topics/916966:Topic:424; see also "The Fifteen Greatest Black Preachers," *Ebony* 49, no. 1 (November 1993).

2. Ibid.

3. Michael Billig, "Psychology, Rhetoric, and Cognition," *History of the Human Sciences* 2, no. 3 (October 19, 1989), 292.

4. Jacqueline Bacon and Glen McClish, "Reinventing the Master's Tools: Nineteenth-century African-American Literary Societies of Philadelphia and Rhetorical Education," *Rhetoric Society Quarterly* 30, no. 4 (Fall 2000), 21.

5. Ibid., 23.

6. Jesse Norman, *Adam Smith: Father of Economics* (New York: Basic Books, 2018), 47.

7. George A. Kennedy, *Classical Rhetoric and Its Christian and Secular Tradition from Ancient to Modern Times*, 2nd ed. (Chapel Hill: University of North Carolina Press, 1999), 278.

8. Ibid.

9. Ibid., 279.

10. Ibid., 280–81.

11. Ibid., 279–80.

12. Ibid., 280.

13. Ibid., 282.

14. In addition, see Duane Liftin, *Public Speaking: A Handbook for Christians* (Grand Rapids, MI: Baker Books, 1992), 40. Liftin says:

> One would be hard pressed to find better instances of such audience adaptation than the messages delivered by the apostles that are recorded in the Book of Acts. For example, Donald Sunukjian, who studied in detail the messages of the apostle Paul in Acts 13, 17, and 20, states that one of the most prominent features of these messages is Paul's "total adaptation of his message to the particular audience before him." Says Sunukjian of Paul, "Every aspect of his preaching is deliberately suited to the hopes, needs, and understandings of his immediate listeners." The study then proceeds to demonstrate adjustments in theme, structure, supporting material, style, and mood in each of Paul's messages. Sunukjian concludes, "Every choice [Paul] makes is guided by the nature of his immediate audience, and every aspect of his preaching is suited to their unique needs."

15. Hugh Blair, "Means of Improving in Eloquence," in Lectures on Rhetoric and Belles Lettres, *ed. Linda Ferreira-Buckley and S. Michael Halloran, Landmarks in Rhetoric and Public Address (1783; Carbondale: Southern Illinois University Press, 2005), 424–25.*

16. Glen McClish, "William G. Allen's 'Orators and Oratory': Inventional Amalgamation, Pathos, and the Characterization of Violence in African-American Abolitionist Rhetoric," *Rhetoric Society Quarterly* 35, no.1 (Winter 2005), 48.

17. Hugh Blair, "Eloquence, or Public Speaking," in *Lectures on Rhetoric and Belles Lettres*, ed. Linda Ferreira-Buckley and S. Michael Halloran, Landmarks in Rhetoric and Public Address (1783; Carbondale: Southern Illinois University Press, 2005), 167–68.

18. Jacqueline Bacon, *The Humblest May Stand Forth: Rhetoric, Empowerment, and Abolition* (Columbia: University of South Carolina Press, 2002), 14.

19. Kennedy, *Classical Rhetoric*, 282.

20. James Monroe Gregory and W. S. Scarborough, *Frederick Douglass, the Orator: Containing an Account of His Life* (Springfield, MA: Willey, 1893), 8–9.

21. Norman, *Adam Smith*, xi.

22. Blair, "Eloquence, or Public Speaking," 163.

23. Norman, *Adam Smith*, 9. Norman says:

In *The Wealth of Nations* Smith praises Scotland's system of parish schools, contrasting them favourably with the less than universal charity schools in England; and he must have had his own burgh schooling partly in mind. He expresses regret that Latin was preferred to elementary geometry and mechanics, but he was sufficiently well schooled in the classics himself to be later excused the remedial first year of the Glasgow University curriculum.

24. Winifred Bryan Horner, "Introduction," in *Scottish Rhetoric and Its Influences*, ed. Lynee Lewis Gaillet (Atlanta: Georgia State University Press, 1998), 4.

25. Ibid.

26. Bacon and McClish, "Reinventing the Master's Tools," 22.

27. Ibid., 31–32.

28. Jacqueline Bacon, *The Humblest May Stand Forth*, 169.

29. Ibid.

30. Richard Lischer, *The Preacher King: Martin Luther King Jr. and the Word That Moved America* (Oxford: Oxford University Press, 1995), 167.

31. Chaim Perelman and Lucie Olbrechts-TyTeca, *The New Rhetoric: A Treatise on Argumentation* (Notre Dame, IN: University of Notre Dame Press, 1971), 189.

32. Billig, "Psychology, Rhetoric, and Cognition," 292. Billig writes:

The image or rhetoric is expressed in its champion's boasts and its opponents' fears, is essentially monologic. There is one speaker, the skilled orator, who delivers the powerful words. The audience, captured by these words, has no speech to make, but reacts with tears, cheers, and helpless admiration. As such there is no dialogic argument, for the message passes unstoppably from the speaker's lips into the audience's brain.

33. Gardner C. Taylor, "A Cry for Guidance," in *The Words of Gardner Taylor*, comp. Edward L. Taylor, vol. 2: *Sermons from the Middle Years, 1970–1980* (Valley Forge, PA: Judson Press, 2000), 23.

34. Ibid.

35. Ibid., 25.

36. Ibid., 26.

37. Kenneth Burke, *On Symbols and Society*, ed. and with an introduction by Joseph R. Gusfield (Chicago: University of Chicago Press, 1989), 9.

38. Gorgias, quoted in Kennedy, *Classical Rhetoric*, 35.

39. Gardner C. Taylor, "Reflections on the Preaching Responsibility," in *The Words of Gardner Taylor*, comp. Edward L. Taylor, vol. 5: *Lectures, Essays, and Interviews* (Valley Forge, PA: Judson Press, 2001), 100.

3
From Where Do Sermons Come?
The Art of Invention

*From where do sermons come? There are perhaps few preachers who
have not pondered this question . . . There may be some rare exceptions
among us, but most preachers will discover that the word God gives us
to utter will not often be by the direct revelation of open heavens and the
thunder of God's own voice spoken to us in the English language and in
the accent of our particular region . . . Most of us discover that sermons
are born of a mysterious romance between preparation and inspiration.*
—Gardner C. Taylor

For sermon whisperers, Gardner Taylor's art of invention, the
second element of rhetoric, is not easily determined. We make
this claim in part because Taylor's mastery of the art of eloquence
made his sermonic discourse move forward without interruptions.
We describe Taylor's preaching then as sermonic discourse, though
not exclusively (there are times when grammar and sentence structure lend themselves simply to sermon). Taylor's preaching can be
made to sound, for some, like a statesman arguing in a parliamen-
tary debate. Therefore, his preaching can be identified with those
who understood and utilized rhetorical devices and rules in order to
communicate in what we can think of as transformative discourse.

Transformative discourse is like that of Lincoln at Gettysburg and Douglass in Corinthian Hall in Rochester, New York. We continue to study, debate, and discuss its impact upon the world for good or ill.

In Taylor's case, his discourse was informed by Christian theology and tradition (as was Lincoln's and Douglass's). Taylor deliberately preached Christian sermons, and by his observing the rules of the classical rhetorical tradition, we see Taylor alongside others like Lincoln and Douglass. We are reminded from chapter 2 that the art of eloquence predominates in Gardner Taylor's sermonic discourse. Proper use of eloquence allowed Taylor to be adroit and to move from introduction to narrative and from it to his argument and his climatic close almost without notice. With this adroitness, which is a character trait of his peculiar manner, he made his sermons unfold like a cannon's burst that is fired strategically to land over its target with symmetrical sheaths.

Keep in mind that his use of eloquence is quilted into all the rhetorical elements available to us (invention, discovery, eloquence or style, memory, and delivery). For this reason, Taylor's invention seems dexterous because it is quilted seamlessly into all aspects of his sacred rhetoric. By sacred rhetoric, we mean preachers who acknowledge the traditions of rhetoric and integrate deliberately the ancient rules into their sermonic discourse. Those who will develop these disciplines will benefit from these elements. Your sermons will be adaptable in diverse settings. This was true of Taylor, and it is one of the significant reasons that his preaching transcends boundaries.

Arranging Arguments:
The Introduction Paragraph

In chapter 2, we made an attempt to highlight Taylor's art of eloquence. We now highlight Taylor's art of invention with the goal that it may improve our understanding of what makes an effective invention. This is similar to the view of Edward P. J. Corbett and Robert J. Connors: "*Inventio* [invention] was concerned with a system or method for finding arguments."[1] We do this by adding supportive helpers that further make an argument shiny and attractive. This is the role of the art of invention; it expands the original idea throughout the entire discourse. That is, its title, subject, thesis, and proposition—the parts of the whole composition—shape and form the substance of a persuasive argument. Each part fits together to inform and make the whole.

At the outset, then, the art of invention is the beginning of the discovery of arguments, which is the organization or arrangement of arguments. Our original idea (the significant feature of the art of invention) is best presented in a single, narrow sentence. Invention, which is the original idea, is the point of departure for the aforementioned parts that help us to discover how to construct the persuasive nature of an argument. It is the vital part of a sermonic discourse. What follows is making known our thesis. Sometimes a thesis is expressed in an entire introductory paragraph (which we prefer), but like the original idea, it is preferable that a thesis is clearly introduced in a single sentence. We suggest, however, that a thesis sentence be broader than the original idea's sentence. What we will discover later, however, is that Gardner Taylor was capable of contracting all of these parts into a single sentence.

For most preachers and other orators, as we previously suggested, a thesis sentence should appear in what can be called simply an introduction paragraph. An introduction paragraph with a discourse's thesis embedded usually is accompanied with a commonplace (later in this chapter, we will address the commonplace separately). Here we define a commonplace as a topic that may be commonly recognized. Next, we suggest that a proposition be included in order to support and reinforce the argument of our discourse's thesis. An argument is plausible because somewhere in the discourse, adroitly in Taylor's case, we have heard it before in a short burst! We have heard it in the original idea.

As mentioned, an introduction paragraph often features a rephrasing of the original idea in a discourse's title and subject, which for a preacher's sermonic discourse is more often than not a biblical text that is to be expounded. What follows is a thesis, proposition, and the claim that will be known as the discourse's argument. This is the seamless quilt. What has not been overly mentioned to this point is the organization and arrangement of a discourse's arguments, which is a simpler way to define what a discovery of arguments means.

What follows is a definition for what we mean by invention, which others call arrangement (also known as discovery):

> Arrangement is the second part of rhetoric, or the second activity of the speaker. Now equipped with the subject matter for your argument or speech—having determined the issue at hand, thought out appropriate supporting arguments drawn from the sources of proof, and identified commonplaces through which to present these arguments—it is time to arrange or organize your speech appropriately into parts.[2]

Rather than separate supporting arguments, we prefer that a single argument be quilted seamlessly into the entire discourse at strategic places, perhaps supported by an illustrative commonplace.

What we have determined to be invention, this preceding definition defines as arrangement or organization. We chose to underline invention in this way because it helps us to understand that the art of invention overlaps and is in continuous support of other elements of rhetoric; everyone does not see these elements in the same way. Third, we take notice of these salient points that reinforce our claim. That is, arrangement or invention has a significant role to play in developing a coherent sermonic discourse. For preachers, the subject matter that is described in our definition is a biblical text. A subject matter (biblical text) is persuasive when it possesses appropriate commonplaces that underscore appropriate aspects of the discourse's argument. Usually proofs are syllogistic logical phrases ($a = b$, $b = c$, $a = c$) that double down and drive the rational and reason of an argument.

Gardner Taylor understood this about arrangement, as will be clearly presented later in this book, particularly in chapter 4, which addresses the prominent role that word arrangement and organization have in the art of style. For now, our objective is highlighting Taylor's use of all the elements of rhetoric to build his sermonic discourses. Keep in mind that Taylor's employment of the art of eloquence is predominating in his use of sacred rhetoric. His art of invention appears in adroit fashion.

Thus, Taylor's sacred rhetoric then belongs to the ages because he mastered the ancient art of eloquence. His eloquence then transcends theological boundaries and sociopolitical and cultural constructs.[3]

We reemphasize that Taylor's eloquence created rhetorical space that is necessary for those who make truth claims. Of course, this space is created for helping all preachers make their arguments persuasive. Remember, Taylor's eloquence reinforces his arguments which, we repeat, are beautiful to hear. It is akin to Hugh Blair's timeless defense for learning the art of eloquence: "True eloquence is the art of placing truth in the most advantageous light for conviction and persuasion."[4]

In addition, what we can determine about Taylor's mastery of the art of eloquence is that he understood that eloquence does not preclude other important parts of discourse development but indeed enhances a discourse's persuasiveness, symmetry, and beauty. In this instance, we can point to Taylor's understanding and his utilization of the art of invention. The art of invention is crucial to the coherence of a sermonic discourse. For him, there exists a "mysterious romance between preparation and inspiration." Furthermore, what is transparent, Taylor's sermon invention begins with finding an original idea.

It is this original idea that he uses to form the persuasiveness of his thesis, which points forward and underlines his argument. The argument then points backward and underlines his thesis and his original idea, which is usually unconcealed in his title. Like the art of eloquence, the art of invention is not learned immediately. It is learned over time but with intentional and deliberate attention; we will come to appreciate its importance for building our discourse's arguments.

Thus, as our appreciation for the function of invention continues to grow, preachers will continue to grow. Even more, preachers: we will become more effective communicators. Effectiveness here means that like Taylor, we too can take advantage of how the art of invention is a connector to a coherent discourse's proverbial dots (which are the five elements of rhetoric). In so many words, connected dots become a method which helps us make persuasive arguments. Remember it is the original idea and the other parts of a discourse that reinforce a well-crafted argument. We shall see Taylor does this in part by employing precise words that create markers which point listeners forward and toward his argument that makes his vision visible, plain, and written upon the hearts of humanity.

Setting Forth a Vision

A sermonic discourse must have a vison, meant here to be guideposts that define for listeners the distance and direction that we will travel with our preachers and congregations on our sermonic journeys. Thus Taylor helps us to understand that invention is an effective helper that is employed to highlight a clear path for congregants to see the preacher's vision. Once again, the vision is underlined and highlighted in the substance of the argument. We remember that an argument's function is to persuade listeners to consider truth claims made by an orator, or in this case, a preacher. A preacher's argument is used to proclaim the Word of God thoroughly and persuasively in order to encourage people to repent and align themselves with Jesus of Nazareth, and the kingdom of God and its principles. This is consistent with Taylor's approach to proclaiming the Word of God.

From Taylor's first words spoken in his discourses, we see that his word choices and arrangements are strategic, intentional, and deliberate, moving his congregations toward casting their approval over his argument's plausibility. "In these matters," Taylor once wrote, "one must not attempt to be overly dogmatic because at its highest the sermon is art, if by that term is meant setting forth of a vision. In such matters of art, creativity and innovation are vital."[5] Thus Taylor helps us to understand that invention—that is, the original idea—is an effective helper that we employ to highlight a clear path for congregants to see the preacher's vision. Indeed, a global positioning system (GPS) orients the audience throughout the sermonic discourse's vision. It is the GPS that informs our understanding, acceptance, and approval of the argument that makes pleasurable what we have heard.

The notion that preachers provide a global positioning system did not originate with Taylor but more than likely with John Henry Jowett. Jowett delivered the Beecher Lectures in 1912 at Yale, where he is quoted to have said, "No sermon is ready for preaching, not ready for writing out, until we can express its theme in a short, pregnant sentence as clear as crystal."[6] By theme, we understand Jowett to mean a well-developed, coherent, concise, and clear thesis that will be supported by a proposition statement or sentence. From this point of departure, sermons bloom and become mature works of art and beauty; beyond the aesthetics, a preacher's mature sermons have a goal to open a window with a clear vision.

Taylor added something similar: "Perhaps it is not going too far to apply this principle to the sermon subject. To the extent that it can be done, the sermon title ought to be a contraction of the theme [thesis, proposition, and introduction paragraph], which in turn ought to attempt to be the sermon concealed, as the sermon ought to be the title revealed."[7] We consider a theme, a thesis, and a subject to be interchangeable descriptions, which is a connecter between a sermonic discourse's introduction and its argument or arguments. Again, we think of this as quilter's pattern threaded seamlessly throughout the quilt.

We add that a thesis sentence is central to an effective introduction, which is usually presented in the body of the introduction paragraph. This is critically important to building a sermon. We suggest if this is done tastefully and artfully, it leads to the discovery of a topic which is first noticed with the use of a commonplace. Think of commonplace as an opening illustration that connects all parts of a discourse. Think too, all parts are not likely to appear in every sermonic discourse evenly, unevenly, or at all. It is only conventional to construct an introduction paragraph in this way. Remember we are advocates. It is merely that preachers use this as a general guide, a roadmap of sorts. This imaginary roadmap serves as a way to order, arrange, and give shape to any sermonic discourse.

Hugh Blair made similar claims about the importance of order and arrangement in public discourse, and we find that Blair's views are akin to those of Taylor. Blair writes, "Order of one kind or other is, indeed essential to every good discourse; that is, everything should be so arranged as that what goes before, may give light and force to what follows. But this may be accomplished by means of a concealed method. What we call division is, when the method is propounded in form to the hearers."[8] As previously mentioned, order and arrangement serve as a guide and roadmap so that we may follow the direction of a sermonic discourse.

Blair means there are two major methods used to organize and arrange a discourse. The first is a method that does not overly enunciate the time, direction, and distance to be traveled over the course of a discourse. Instead it deliberately conceals what we consider to be mental quilt squares that which makes us run ahead of the discourse's arguments. Therefore, we see this method as a guard against that which makes a sermonic discourse too predictable if not boring and unrepairable to listeners. What is more, we contend that concealment avoids interruptions that may hinder a listener's appreciation for the art of preaching and particularly preaching that is informed by the art of eloquence. This method is effective for those who are adept at understanding that word pictures, for example, are carefully organized and arranged to enhance our "feel" for a sermon discourse.

The second method makes organized and arranged divisions the focus in a discourse. We more clearly understand divisions as partitions, which appear between parts of a discourse to make it seemingly slow down for comprehension and reflection. Said in another way, partitions slow the pace of the sermon's action. Perhaps partitions are built into a discourse in order to give listeners signs and markers, which provide to them relief and assurance that a discourse under their consideration will not continue as an unyielding and detached oration. It is possible that partitions add protection for listeners from the enduring burdens, weariness, tediousness, and, sadly, emotional exhaustion.

Archbishop Cambray understood an audience's fear of an unyielding discourse with no apparent end in sight. As an example, he wrote in his *Dialogues on Eloquence* that the use of sermon partitions or divisions was "a modern intervention; that it was never practiced by the Fathers of the Church; and, what is certainly true, that it took rise from the schoolmen, when metaphysics began to be introduced into preaching."[9]

Blair writes that Cambray did not value the presence of sermon partitions or divisions. Instead he felt a partition to be "stiff; [and] that it breaks the unity of the discourse." Regarding what Blair writes of the archbishop's resistance to a sermon's (discourse's) divisions, we have noticed similar resistance or at the least its absence in sermon discourses of Taylor. Indeed, we have noticed that he avoids partitions or divisions in his sermon discourse:

> More often than not, the structure of a sermon can be determined by
> the movement of the text itself. Some of us like to look upon the ser-

mon as a journey. We start with some sense of [a] goal: To what part of the life in Christ is it that we want to point and lead the worshipers? We then seek a point of origin and a path, roadway, by which we hope to arrive at the city that is the destination of that sermon's pilgrimage. Incidentally, this concept can greatly assist those who would like to develop some skill in preaching without [a] manuscript.[10]

Taylor's emphasis was on the art of eloquence, not on this part of the science of preaching, which here means partitions or divisions. Let us reiterate Taylor envisioned a sermon as a journey, a goal to be reached, a point of origin (which is another way to describe an original idea), a path, a roadway, a destination and pilgrimage. If we characterize Taylor's pulpit work as akin to that which Cambray promoted, we can characterize partitions and divisions as detours, closed roads, and the like.

In short, Taylor describes a sermonic discourse as an organic movement. His sermons grew out commonplaces, the biblical text in light of current cultural norms, and contextual spaces with which people may be familiar. By approaching the preaching task in this manner, Taylor's discourses remain in constant motion, always moving forward and taking his listeners somewhere he foresees and gradually unconceals.

To be sure, Taylor strategically concealed full view of his discourse's ultimate goals along the journey so that his listeners would remain constantly on the edge of their seats, and while there, he held his listeners in a shroud of mystery. Like Cambray, Taylor's sermon discourse did not permit interruptions made by partitions or divisions. Taylor's sermons then were a work of art that should not be disturbed but entered into and appreciated.

Blair, however, did not hold to this view. Instead, he insisted that quality sermon discourse is to be instructive in order for listeners to understand biblical texts. When this occurs, it leads to edification of the whole (for the preacher and the listeners). For Blair, this is the primary goal. That is, a preacher's chief responsibility is providing simple truth claims for people to consider and understand.

What is more, Blair responds to Cambray's resistance to partitions: "I cannot help being of opinion, that the present method of dividing a Sermon into heads, ought not to be laid aside . . . The heads of a Sermon are of great assistance to the memory and recollection of a hearer."[11] Blair, who was once the Regius Professor of Rhetoric and Belles Lettres at the University of Edinburgh, supported the use of headings (partitions).

When properly used, partitions forewarn and orient an audience to the sermonic discourse's current location and direction traveled, and when we have arrived at our destination, we have arrived together. There is merit to Blair's perspective, and surely his professional dedication and spiritual giftedness lend themselves to an expert's informed opinion. We, however, agree with Cambray's understanding of sermonic discourse. Without partitions and divisions, we find that sermonic discourses are less cumbersome and stiff. Certainly this was the way of Taylor; his sermons avoided commercial interruptions, stops, and starts.

Taylor avoided sluggish, heavily weighted impediments that might have moved his listeners from the scenes and word pictures that he crafted and delivered to them. Taylor followed the rules of discourse, but like all great platform and pulpit speakers, he knew when and how to bend rhetorical rules, as we shall see later. Taylor's discourse organization and arrangement were laden and hidden in plain sight of his audiences. We contend that this was accomplished because Taylor's arts of eloquence and invention were quilted seamlessly together.

Finding Appropriate Arguments

What is furthermore determined, Taylor's original idea helps us to make an attempt to assign a method to him, something that will help us describe if not explain his creative genius. According to Cicero, "the speaker relied on native genius, on method of art, or on diligence to help find appropriate arguments." Obviously, someone who had a native, intuitive sense for proper arguments was at a great advantage. But lacking such an endowment, a person could have recourse either to dogged industry or to some system for finding arguments.[12]

Following Cicero's lead, we characterize Taylor's creativity as an indication of his native genius. That is, Taylor possessed the method of art to find appropriate arguments. Another way of thinking about Taylor's creativity is that he followed the way of persons who do not possess "a native, intuitive sense for proper arguments."

Indeed, Taylor did not rely solely upon his native genius. Instead, he employed something that we find similar to Cicero's "dogged industry or some system for finding arguments." Whether or not preachers are endowed with rare native genius, which is a high level of creativity, all preachers will benefit by finding a reliable method to improve our original sermon idea. Where then does the sermon's original idea originate?

Imagine Taylor (or any other preacher) as a skillful prosecutor. Obviously this woman or man is ethical and is possessed of the integrity and ability to scrutinize all available evidence to formulate her or his arguments. Sound and plausible arguments then begin with interrogation and prosecution of "revelant" and "relevant" materials. In this instance, all available evidence begins with biblical texts.

We admit that an original idea may be informed from other sources, such as social environs and disciplines (e.g., reading, walking in a park, listening to music). These are hermeneutic cues.[13] We assert this was part of Taylor's peculiar manner. That is, "whatever [the sermon] structure, a sermon must deal with two things: the 'revelant' (to use Kyle Haselden's fine term) and 'relevant.'"[14] Taylor found homiletic jewels hidden in plain sight, in Haselden's intentional play on words. These words point us toward available evidence and how that evidence is presented to congregations and made clear.

Taylor understood that Haselden's sermon invention or original idea comes into view when we make observations from the world in which we live and the texts that we study. We then look to make contrasts and comparisons between our biblical and contemporary worldviews. That is, like a prosecutor, Taylor takes into consideration all available evidence.

This we associate with Haselden's method, which is a nexus between God's revelation of biblical texts and the relatedness of contemporary listeners, that is, that which informs and influences people in our contemporary contexts. Thus biblical texts grew from ancient contexts, cultures, and events that became a canon that was shaped over a course of two millennia. Let us add that these texts were episodes revealed by God's Spirit and Presence. This is the point of departure for Haselden's "revelant." The first step is to believe that God is, and that God reveals what Haselden called "relevant"—that which we call reality.

Although biblical texts are complex compilations of poetry, narratives, and literary, theological, and historical writings, each has withstood diverse critiques, criticisms, and the test of time. We then do not compromise our process that demands prosecutorial interrogation of available evidence. It becomes our task, however, to make it understandable to postmodern and postresurrection audiences. In so many words, what may be accepted historically as something that happened, or something that was written in ancient times, does not mean necessarily that audiences can relate to its claims without the preacher's help. Time and distance make this difficult. Biblical texts record events that are ancient in comparison with current events within our contemporary cultures. Therefore other considerations must come into view.

Preachers must consider the best ways to communicate their vision that does not compromise the antiquity of revealed religion's sacred texts, which is the revelant. At the same time, the sermon vision must make all available evidence relatable or relevant homiletically in contemporary terms to contemporary audiences. In short, this implies that there is an intersection between then and now, revelant and relevant. It is this intersection on which Taylor relied to create his original idea. It is the connector that helps him to prosecute his discourse's argument. We view this intersection of disciplines as an important key for us to understand the art of eloquence that possessed Taylor.

Identifying the Parts of an Introduction Paragraph

Thus far, we have laid out a roadmap that covers much composition, rhetoric, and homiletic terrain. In this chapter, we began with Taylor's use of the art of invention, which we renamed as an original idea. Like Taylor, we contend that the original idea contracts into a sermon discourse's title, subject, thesis, proposition, and argument.

We remember, however, that Taylor's original idea was adroitly presented and quilted seamlessly into all aspects of his discourse. Taylor is a master of this art, but such an art is learned over time. We now attempt to identify these essential but separate parts which are presented together in an introduction paragraph.

Because of familiarity and to maintain uniformity, we return to "Seeing Our Hurts with God's Eyes" (John 15:1), which we highlighted in chapter 1. In the first instance, we did so to become conversant with Taylor's use of the art of eloquence. In the second instance and here, it is used to underline and locate the aforementioned parts that are quilted into an introduction paragraph.

As was previously mentioned, often Taylor used vivid word pictures in order to "get into the pew." This is another way to say that Taylor crafted creatively his introductions to bring collectively, and vicariously, his audiences into the discourse's scene. Typically, his introductions are lengthier than what other preachers may present. Later in this chapter, we will address Taylor's craft to build an introduction which is located in his ability to use a commonplace for this very purpose. We believe that we can make this simple to grasp.

Let us imagine that we see Gardner Taylor standing in a pulpit and gazing into a sea of faces. He is wearing an unbuttoned black robe with three black embroidered shoulder chevrons that are nearly unnoticeable at a distance. What is noticed is his academic hood bleeding in crimson which is draped over his robe and his black three-piece suit. He acknowledges the choir's musical rendition, which was presented as a sermon preparatory hymn. He announces his sermonic discourse's title, "Seeing Our Hurts with God's Eyes." We are in awe of his baritone voice as he reads his subject: "I am the true vine, and my Father is the husbandman" (John 15:1, King James Version). He begins his sermon with a protracted commonplace to highlight his orchestrated sense of compatibility between his title and subject.

Here is an example of how Taylor uses a commonplace to attract his listeners' attention to his discourse's subject and thesis and eventually his argument. We will expand our definition of a commonplace later in this chapter (the commonplace is the entirety of the first excerpted paragraph), but as previously stated, let us think of it as Taylor's opening illustration. Once again, Taylor knew how to "get into the pew." Understandably, many people who were assembled had experienced some if not all of the emotions that we attach to his descriptive word pictures that point to our traumatic experiences.

Second, and adroitly (in the second excerpted paragraph), Taylor masterfully moves from that which is commonly shared by most, by adroitly contracting his original idea, title, subject, thesis, proposition, and argument into a single sentence. (It is rare and difficult to do this, but with gift and experience on his side, Taylor does so.) To support his contracted sentence, Taylor assures his audience that no one in attendance should feel paranoid about their shared emotional trauma. Instead, he reinforces that trauma is commonly shared and universally experienced by the entirety of the human family.

Over a course of minutes, Taylor began to unfold one of his sermon masterpieces, and we will immediately appreciate his arts of eloquence, invention, and word pictures that connect us to its penetrating substance:

> If I were to survey this magnificent congregation tonight to take a listing, a poll of the psychic bruises, the spiritual hurts that are abroad across this grand congregation, how many reports of deep inner hurt would come back—how many apprehensions, how many anxieties, how many misgivings, how many fears, how many disappointments, how many betrayals, how much love unrequited? What a mountain it would make! If I could take a poll tonight of all the scars that are represented here, stretched out before my face, what a mountain it would make. Sickness endured, sickness feared, the loss of those whom we have loved, miscalculations about our ambitions, the frustrations of our hopes, the brokenness of our dreams, the unmet ambitions—what a mountain.
>
> *Perhaps in thinking about our hurts we attach too much importance to what happens to us rather than looking at the results of the things that happen to us, for what is really grievous is not what happens but how it affects us.* That is the meaning of panic, too, of not knowing what to do under this circumstance or under that, of feeling caged, trapped, cornered, helpless. Here is the difference, I am sure, between how a Christian views the things that happen in his or her life and how the person [who] is not a Christian views the things that happen in his or her life. It is not that the same things do not happen;

it is that in a Christian spirit, they are seen in a different way. For the Lord makes his rain to fall, as he does his sun to shine upon the just as well as the unjust. But there is a difference with which righteous and the unrighteous receive the rain. The unrighteous farmer, seeing the rain fall when it is needed, is likely to figure it was about time. The unrighteous, to some extend at least, complains. The righteous farmer is likely to look up to the heavens and thank God that the rains came.[15]

Taylor has demonstrated his mastery over the arts of eloquence, invention, and word pictures. Of peculiar import, we focus our attention on a single sentence: "Perhaps in thinking about our hurts [instead of feeling our hurts] we attach too much importance to what happens to us rather than looking at the results of the things that happen to us, for what is really grievous is not what happens but how it affects us." Taylor has connected his original idea and title to his subject; his subject to his thesis; his thesis to his proposition; and his proposition to his argument. His argument points backward toward his original idea.

Taylor's argument is brilliant. In order to reinforce his argument, Taylor now employs proofs, which we defined earlier as syllogistic logical sentences: "Here is the difference," he said, "I am sure, between how a Christian views the things that happen in his or her life and how the person [who] is not a Christian views the things that happen in his or her life. It is not that the same things do not happen [to us]; it is that in a Christian spirit, they are seen in a different way." In short, Christians and unbelievers differ in how each perceives and responds to their emotional trauma. Immediately we notice that Taylor has dramatized these differences by moving his audience's attention from its collective emotions and replaced emotion with an eloquent appeal to reason.

What has taken place? Taylor has captured his audience's emotions with word pictures, and then adroitly he uses what is called juxtaposition. Taylor reorganizes and rearranges these associated facts (emotions and reason) and places the highest value on the importance of reason. That is, Taylor replaces his audience's old perception, which is primarily an emotional response, with a new perception, one which is primarily rational.

This is the concealed subject and the original idea, namely, his original premise which was once concealed but by his use of juxtaposition is now unconcealed. This points us toward his brilliant understanding of organization and arrangement. He has moved his audience's emotional perceptions and responses toward a new subject, which is rational perceptions and responses.

Now the rational is the subject, the victor, and the attractive. Conversely, the emotion is objectified, or the object, and is unattractive. In this way, Taylor has connected his title, subject, thesis, proposition, and argument by contracting each into a single sentence. Finally, we must wait on Taylor's single sentence to see how and where his sermonic discourse's original idea is quilted into the whole. Now his original idea is made visible not only in the single sentence but also in the title "Seeing Our Hurts with God's Eyes": "Perhaps in thinking about our hurts we attach too much importance to what happens to us rather than looking at the results."

As promised, we now intend to define thoroughly what a commonplace is. We have made a decision to address it here, based on its import to discourse and narrowly to that of Taylor. Undeniably a commonplace has a large role in Taylor's style, particularly in his sermon discourse's introductions. (The art of style is the subject of the next chapter. There we will discuss and demonstrate comprehensively its presence in all verifiable forms of discourses.) Commonplace is referred to as topics. "By . . . topics, I mean the propositions peculiar to any given discipline, by general topics those that are common to all."[16] An effective use of commonplaces or topics will aid all preachers' effective use of her and his use of an original idea, thesis, propositions, and arguments.

A commonplace for Taylor was used to build interest in his sermonic discourse; also for him, commonplaces served as a compass for where he was to take his listeners on their shared sermonic journey. Richard Lischer described Taylor's employment of commonplaces as a significant aspect of his oratorical power. "Taylor . . . [was] trained in . . . rhetorical tricks—the ponderous beginning, the vowels distended three times their normal length, the affected stutter—and [was] adroit at manipulating inherited commonplaces."[17]

Corbett and Connors define commonplace or topic as "the method that classical rhetoricians devised to aid the speaker in discovering matter for the three modes of appeal [ethos, logos, and pathos] . . . These [commonplaces] are so called because they constitute regions of experience from which the substance [art of invention] of an argument can be drawn. It is a matter of everyday observation that arguments are made."[18] By regions of experience, we can make our understanding of it simple. It is that which influences our understanding of how we feel and think about our world and our lives in our world. Regions of experience point toward our formal and informal education, social and political worldviews, sociological environments and other cultural influences, and personal and collective experiences.

These regions of experience then make a commonplace a rhetorical device that helps preachers to predict how, where, and when many persons will find our illustrative material plausible. This is because those persons have witnessed, experienced, and identified similarities with our claims made. In short, commonplaces create intersections of collective experiences commonly witnessed in a congregation.

Remember, the commonplace is not a poll or a survey taken, but it is a powerful and effective way to demonstrate empathy with listeners. It is a way for listeners to build trust with the preacher who has demonstrated rhetorically that she or he identifies with the listeners' human conditions. In this way, the metaphoric word picture that Taylor employs helped his listeners to imagine that if a poll or survey were taken, the content more than likely would be confirmed as if a scientific method was used to retrieve accurate information from them.

Taylor's sermonic discourse "Seeing Our Hurts with God's Eyes" is a clear example for how to use a commonplace. He will use Corbett's and Connor's commonplace's "regions of experience," and in this way, he infuses a commonplace into his introduction:

If I were to survey this magnificent congregation tonight to take a listing, a poll of the psychic bruises, the spiritual hurts that are abroad across this grand congregation, how many reports of deep inner hurt would come back—how many apprehensions, how many misgivings, how many fears, how many disappointments, how many betrayals, how much love unrequited? What a mountain it would make! If I could take a poll tonight of all the scars that are represented here, stretched out before my face, what a mountain it would make. Sickness endured, sickness feared, the loss of those whom we have loved, miscalculations about our ambitions, the frustrations of our hopes, the brokenness of our dreams, the unmet ambitions—what a mountain.[19]

We suggest that Taylor's sermonic discourse's introduction is near to what Lischer previously asserted. Taylor's introduction begins with and sustains a ponderous beginning and rhetorical tricks. We reaffirm here, Taylor is a master of the art of eloquence and, we add, invention. We too point toward Corbett's and Connor's definition of commonplaces as "regions of experience."

In the previous excerpt, Taylor has drawn on his audience's collective emotional trauma. Taylor knows that if a "listing" or a "poll" would have been taken, the majority of listeners undoubtedly would have experienced several of those "psychic bruises." Here is a brilliant example of how a commonplace works in a sermonic discourse.

There are other ways to arrange and organize the parts of a sermon discourse (original idea, subject, thesis, proposition, and argument) than the one that we advocate. Samuel DeWitt Proctor organized and arranged these parts differently (proposition, subject, antithesis) in his sermons.[20] In fact, he suggested in *The Certain Sound of the Trumpet* that Taylor's sermon introductions begin with an antithesis instead of thesis (paragraph) in an introduction paragraph:

> I learned this listening to the sermons of Harry Emerson Fosdick while in seminary. I was trying to recover my belief system after a shattering introduction to biblical studies. As Dr. Fosdick began—always with a challenging, searching antithesis—he had my attention from the first sentence to the very end. Dr. Taylor does the same now, with one exception: he holds his listeners in a longer antithesis than usual.[21]

Proctor's image is among those faces chiseled into the Mount Rushmore of preachers. Of course, Gardner Taylor is alongside him. It is difficult to disagree with Proctor on any account, but we do here. It is not observation of the length of Taylor's introduction with which we disagree; there we wholeheartedly agree. We disagree with Proctor in this way: we do not affirm that the introductions of Taylor's sermonic discourses are revealed in an antithesis. Instead, we stick to our claim that Taylor begins his sermonic discourses with an introduction paragraph with his thesis in tow.

We keep in mind, Taylor wrote the foreword of Proctor's aforementioned book and made a claim that we believe supports our prerogative: "As to his Hegelian structure for sermons, it is certainly one of the sound methods of sermon construction, though not by any means the only one. Having filed that caveat, one would necessarily add that the writer is on target in his insistence on 'thesis.'"[22]

Taylor did insist on forming and positing a thesis; however, we suggest that he did so in the method that we have presented thus far. Taylor's introduction, however, does hold his audiences longer in suspense, as Proctor correctly describes, before Taylor shifts to his thesis, proposition, and argument. This is his peculiar manner, which now is unconcealed as another way to describe his style.

Style or Taylor's peculiar manner is the subject of our next chapter. We intend to demonstrate how it is a prominent feature in Taylor's narrative development that focuses on his sermonic discourse's primary biblical text. We may remember from chapter 1 that narrative persuades. In order to persuade, Taylor continues his use of arrangement and organization as a significant aspect of his narrative development. We shall see how Taylor's narrative comes to life with word pictures, his proper use of words, phrases, and sentences, and how these are quilted seamlessly together and become full paragraphs that bloom into an attractive composition filled with persuasive arguments that make his work sacred rhetoric. These are important parts of his art of style, which is another way to say that the art of style further refines his peculiar manner.

Epigraph

Gardner C. Taylor, "Contemporary Preaching," in *The Words of Gardner Taylor*, comp. Edward L. Taylor, vol. 5: *Lectures, Essays, and Interviews* (Valley Forge, PA: Judson Press, 2001), 171–72.

NOTES

1. Edward P. J. Corbett and Robert J. Connors, *Classical Rhetoric for the Modern Student*, 4th ed. (Oxford: Oxford University Press, 1999), 132.

2. Marcus Tullius Cicero, *How to Win an Argument: An Ancient Guide to the Art of Persuasion*, ed. James M. May (Princeton, NJ: Princeton University Press, 2016), 40.

3. See chapter 1, An Introduction to the Art of Eloquence," where the reference to Taylor's "peculiar manner" is made.

4. Hugh Blair, "Eloquence of the Pulpit," in *Lectures on Rhetoric and Belles Lettres*, ed. Linda Ferreira-Buckley and S. Michael Halloran, Landmarks in Rhetoric and Public Address (1783; Carbondale: Southern Illinois University Press, 2005), 317. Included here is the entire paragraph of which our direct quote is a part:

> It may perhaps occur to some, that preaching is no proper subject of the art of eloquence. This, it may be said, belongs only to human studies and inventions: but the truths of religion, with the greater simplicity, and the less mixture of art they are set forth, are likely to prove the more successful. This objective would have weight, if eloquence were, as the persons who make such an objection commonly take it, to be, an ostentatious and deceitful art, the stud of words and of plausibility only, calculated to please, and to tickle the ear. But against this idea of eloquence I have all along guarded. True eloquence is the art of placing truth in the most advantageous light for conviction and persuasion. This is what every good man [and woman] who preaches the Gospel not only may, but ought to have at heart. It is most intimately connected with the success of his ministry; and were it needful, as assuredly it is not, to reason any further on this head, we might refer to the discourses of the prophets and apostles, as models of the most sublime and persuasive eloquence, adapted both to the imagination and the passions of men.

5. Gardner C. Taylor, "Titles," in *The Words of Gardner Taylor*, comp. Edward L. Taylor, vol. 5: *Lectures, Essays, and Interviews* (Valley Forge, PA: Judson Press, 2001), 38–39.

6. Ibid., 38.

7. Ibid., 39.

8. Hugh Blair, "Conduct of a Discourse in All Its Parts—Introduction—Division—Narration and Explication," in *Lectures on Rhetoric and Belles Lettres*, ed. Linda Ferreira-Buckley and S. Michael Halloran, Landmarks in

Rhetoric and Public Address (1783; Carbondale: Southern Illinois University Press, 2005), 350.

> After the Introduction, what commonly comes next in order, is the proposition, or enunciation of the subject: concerning which there is nothing to be said, but that it should be as clear and distinct as possible, and expressed in few and plain words, without the least affectation. To this generally succeeds the Division, or the laying down the method of the discourse; . . . I do not mean, that in a formal division or distribution of it into parts, is requisite. There are many occasions of public speaking when this is neither requisite nor would be proper; when the discourse, perhaps, is to be short, or only one point is to be treated of: or when the speaker does choose to warn his hearers of the method he is to follow, or of the conclusion to which he seeks to bring them. Order of one kind or other is, indeed essential to every good discourse; that is, everything should be so arranged as that what goes before, may give light and force to what follows. But this may be accomplished by means of a concealed method. What we call division is, when the method is propounded in form to the hearers.

9. Ibid. The full paragraph reads:

> The discourse in which this sort of division most commonly takes place, is a Sermon; and a question has been moved, whether this method of laying down heads, as it is called, be the best method of preaching. A very able judge, the Archbishop of Cambray, in his Dialogues on Eloquence, declares strongly against it. He observes, that it is a modern invention; that it was never practiced by the fathers of the church; and, what is certainly true, that it took its rise from the schoolmen, when metaphysics began to be introduced into preaching. He is of [the] opinion, that it renders a sermon stiff; that it breaks the unity of the discourse; and that, by the natural connection of one part with another, the attention of the hearers would be carried along the whole with more advantage.

10. Gardner C. Taylor, "Shaping Sermons by the Shape of Text and Preacher," in *The Words of Gardner Taylor*, comp. Edward L. Taylor, vol. 5: *Lectures, Essays, and Interviews* (Valley Forge, PA: Judson Press, 2001), 46. Blair writes in, "Conduct of a Discourse in All Its Parts," 350–51:

> But, notwithstanding his authority and his arguments, I cannot help being of opinion, that the present method of dividing a Sermon into

heads, ought not to be laid aside. Established practice has now given it so much weight, that, were there nothing more in its favor, it would be dangerous for any Preacher to deviate so far from a common track. But the practice itself has also, in my judgement, much reason on its side. If formal partitions give a Sermon less of the oratorical appearance, they render it, however, more clear, more easily apprehended, and, of course, more instructive to the bulk of hearers, which is always the main object to be kept in view. The heads of a Sermon are of great assistance to the memory and recollection of the hearer. They serve also to fix his attention. They enable him more easily to keep pace with the progress of the Discourse: they give him pauses and resting places, where he can reflect on what has been said, and look forward to what is to follow ... With regard to breaking Unity of a Discourse, I cannot be of [the] opinion that there arises, from the quarter, any argument against the method I am defending. If the Unity be broken, it is to the nature of the heads, or topics of which the Speaker treats, that this is to be imputed: not to his laying them down in form. On the contrary, if his heads be well-chosen, his marking them out, and distinguishing them, in place of impairing the Unity of the whole, renders it more conspicuous and complete by showing how all the parts of a Discourse hang upon one another, and tend to one point.

11. Blair, "Conduct of a Discourse in All Its Parts," 350.

12. Corbett and Connors, *Classical Rhetoric for the Modern Student*, 17.

13. Joseph Evans, *Lifting the Veil Over Eurocentrism: The Du Boisian Hermeneutic of Double Consciousness* (Trenton, NJ: Africa World Press, 2014), 15.

14. Gardner C. Taylor, "Contemporary Preaching," in *The Words of Gardner Taylor*, comp. Edward L. Taylor, vol. 5: *Lectures, Essays, and Interviews* (Valley Forge, PA: Judson Press, 2001), 96. Here Taylor provides context for where he heard and understood Haselden's method for developing an effective sermon invention:

Some years ago, Kyle Haselden, who was a West Virginia Baptist, for a little while prior to what many of us thought was an untimely death, [was] editor of *The Christian Century*. During that era, I spent an evening in a Pullman car with him, talking almost all night. He invented a term and used it that night, what he called the "revelant," or that which is given to us, the mighty pronouncements, the great decisive acts of God. He brought that word which he created, "revelant," together with that word which is known to all of us, "relevant." And I take it to be that this is the center of the responsibility for those of us who in one way or another are called to proclaim the Word of God. Our responsibility is to bring that which is given to that which is happening and to have them intersect.

15. Gardner C. Taylor, "Seeing Our Hurts with God's Eyes," in *The Words of Gardner Taylor*, comp. Edward L. Taylor, vol. 2: *Sermons from the Middle Years, 1970–1980* (Valley Forge, PA: Judson Press, 2001), 86.

16. Lane Cooper, *The Rhetoric of Aristotle: An Expanded Translation with Supplementary Examples for Students of Composition and Public Speaking* (London: Prentice-Hall International, 1932), 16.

17. Richard Lischer, *The Preacher King: Martin Luther King Jr. and the Word That Moved America* (Oxford: Oxford University Press, 1995), 41.

18. Edward P. J. Corbett and Robert J. Connors. *Classical Rhetoric for the Modern Student 4th Edition* (Oxford: Oxford University Press, 1999), 19. For those who will appreciate a fuller explanation for how common-places work, we have included this lengthy paragraph:

The method that classical rhetoricians devised to aid the speaker in discovering matter for the three modes of appeal [deliberative oratory, forensic oratory, and epideictic oratory] was topics [commonplaces]. Topics is the English translation of the Greek word *topoi* and the Latin word loci. Literally, topos or locus mean "place or region" (note our words topography and locale). In rhetoric, a topic was a place or store or thesaurus to which one resorted to find something to say on a given subject. More specifically, a topic was a general head or line of argument which suggested material from which proofs could be made. To put it another way, the topics constituted a method of probing one's subject to discover possible ways of developing that subject. Aristotle distinguished two kinds of topics: (1) the special topics (he called them *idioi topoi* or *eide*); (2) the common topics (*koinoi topoi*). The special topics were those classes of argument appropriate to particular kinds of discourse. In other words, they were some kinds of arguments that were used exclusively in law courts; some that were confined to the public forums; others that appeared only in ceremonial addresses. The common topics, on the other hand, were fairly limited stock of arguments that could be used for any occasion or type of speech. Aristotle named four common topics: (1) more or less (the topic of degree); (2) the possible and the impossible; (3) past fact and future fact; (4) greatness and smallness (the topic of size as distinguished from the topic of degree). In the text itself we will see how the topics are put to work.

19. Taylor, "Seeing Our Hurts with God's Eyes," 86.

20. Samuel D. Proctor, *The Certain Sound of the Trumpet: Crafting a Sermon of Authority*, foreword by Gardner C. Taylor (Valley Forge, PA: Judson Press, 1994), 54.

21. Ibid., 69.

22. Ibid., x.

4

His Peculiar Manner
The Art of Style

I urge all preachers to take a single word most seriously. I think that we have seen in preaching in general a sort of de-poeticizing of the language as part of an effort to "dumb down" the content, to make it simple. People don't want to be dumbed down; they want to be lifted up. In regard, I think that we need to recover a sense of preaching as an art form, one that features grand and piercing language, language that wrestles with and grips the hearer. —Gardner C. Taylor

Gardner Taylor possessed, indeed, a peculiar manner. The term "peculiar manner" provides for us a way to grasp Taylor's mystique. A peculiar manner is nothing more than a proper use of a euphemism that is meant to describe style. Thus, a peculiar manner, which is Hugh Blair's term for style, is that which is underneath the orator. What is more, style reveals the orator's character, quality, and depth that we identify with her or his discourse. What then is the connectedness between eloquence and style?

Style or a peculiar manner adds to eloquence. In short, style adds structure through a proper use of language which functions beneath the surface and adds to outer and visible beauty, which is eloquence. Recently, some students and this writer were standing outside of the Interdenominational Theological Center Chapel. There we observed the fault lines in a massive clay flower pot. The fault lines were visible but did not compromise the pot's sturdy structure or its function. Inside the pot were flowers such as marigolds and daffodils. Underneath the flowers was dirt, and underneath the dirt were the flowers' hidden roots that reach deeply into the pot's structure.

All of this provides context to a visible ornamentation which in this instance were the flowers. The pot's visible fault lines made the pot more aesthetically peculiar and interesting and provided rustic character to the flowers and the pot's beauty and function. In fact, without the pot's fault lines, the flowers would not have seemed so lovely. Why? Because the pot's faults lines provide a narrative.

The narrative suggests that the pot has survived many seasons. During different temperatures the pot survives, the pot survives mishandling, and perhaps it survives being dropped carelessly. Nevertheless, it functions and continues to provide a safe space for the flowers' roots to grow deeply, naturally, and undisturbed inside the pot's structure. In short, the pot has an intrinsic style of extrinsic character. Its character helps us to understand its narrative. Symbolically, then, the pot has a story to be told—worth observation. All of this, however, shows the potter's style, character, and craftsmanship.

Well-Crafted Discourse Reveals Character

A pulpit orator too is a craftsman. As a craftsman, she uses her mind to create an image that eventually will become a well-crafted discourse. Second, she crafts a discourse with tools, something similar to a potter's wheel, in order to fashion her discourse. Third, no more than a craftsman can hide or prevent the eventual pot's visible fault lines, neither can the pulpit orator hide or prevent her or his eventual personal fault lines—nor should this happen. Instead, all that has been mentioned provides beauty and function which is to be brought forth in their discourse. The unconcealed fault lines point to the style of character employed to craft the discourse.

In fact, character, even with fault lines, reveals the style of the pulpit orator. At the same time, it reveals the quality and depth of the discourse's character. By this, we mean that character or style points toward the native genius that is necessary to invent and shape the contours and content of any discourse. This enhances our appreciation for style. Style underlines the person's mind behind the orator's depth of character and choice of words. This is a clear sense of style. Style is character. The potted flowers' roots require depth in order to grow; and in a similar fashion, we are able to understand that a pulpit orator's discourse needs depth that shows the quality of a pulpit orator's discourse.

In addition, style shows the person behind the choice. This sense of style surfaces personal character, which lets us add that style showcases the person's passions, convictions, and spiritual and natural gifts. Like the potted flowers' roots that reach deep into the potter's pot, a pulpit orator's discourse reveals style—in character. Without style, we may have difficulty perceiving quality and depth that add structure and function to discourse. Like our clay pot's visible fault lines, which give it a peculiarity, a pulpit orator possesses style of character, which we have claimed is at the center of a peculiar manner.

In order to understand thoroughly a preacher's peculiar manner of style (that is, language spoken out, which reveals quality and depth), we now introduce one of Taylor's most admired sermons, "The Strange Ways of God" (Luke 3:1-2). The sermonic discourse was delivered during a Martin Luther King Jr. memorial service in January 1972 at Harvard University. We keep in mind that the printed words that appear upon pages do not recapture the baritone voice that speaks in the style of a black Victorian pulpit orator preaching out in this structure of language:[1]

> Father Robinson, Pastor Cooper, reverend clergy, my brothers and sisters. How strange is it that, all across this land tonight as we come to the second week of this second year of the seventh decade of the twentieth century, a kind of shiver would pass through the land. A benign shadow seems to rest upon this country. It's a shiver of memory and of hope. How strange that it would be occasioned by the life of a man who did not live to see the fulfillment of his normal span. How strange that this whole land would be affected so deeply and people of so many diverse beliefs and outlooks could come together in some deeply solemn and profoundly religious atmosphere. How strange that it would occur around the life of a man who did not come from a majority people but who came of the loins of a disinherited and disallowed people. And yet this is the strange and anomalous actuality.

From one end of this country to the other beginning tonight, a strange shiver passes through the land, and from one end of the country to the other people begin coming together, warmed by the memory and lighted hope. Four springs and summers have come and gone, and yet this shadow looms larger and more blessed upon the country. His widow in her own queenly manner said but within the last few days that it will be fifty years before the full assessment of the life of Martin King can begin to be made in this country, and it will be.[2]

After Taylor acknowledges the presence of those who shared the pulpit platform, his sermonic discourse begins with a protracted commonplace embedded in his introduction. No fewer than six times, Taylor repeats "how strange" or simply the word *strange* to reemphasize his original idea. Three times, Taylor repeats the word *shiver* to create the kind of mood he wants his audience to feel as he unconceals his sermonic thesis and its connection between "strange" and "shiver." He employs the word *shadow* twice to resurrect King's presence that remains indelibly among us. He uses the word *land* four times and the word *country* five times. Often, these words appear in the same organizational arrangement in order to dramatize his argument: "a strange shiver passes through the land, and from one end of the country to the other people begin coming together."[3] Notice in the next excerpt a deliberate thematic pattern that reveals the connectedness between the words *strange*, *shiver*, *land*, *shadow*, and *country*: "How strange is it that, all across this land tonight as we come to the second week of the second year of the seventh decade of the twentieth century, a kind of shiver would pass through the land. A benign shadow seems to rest upon this country. It's a shiver of memory and of hope."[4]

This example is a clear and neat usage of words that undergird that which we previously introduced as the structure of language, its beauty, and how it functions: "his embellishment [eloquence], by means of musical cadence, figures, or other parts of speech" defines his style.[5] Later in this chapter, we will reconsider how words, phrases, and sentence arrangements add quality and depth to the substance of style.

Taylor's rhetorical strategy follows closely that which Hugh Blair once wrote about the manner of style:

When I entered on the consideration of style, I observed that words being the copies of our ideas, there must always be a very intimate connection between the manner in which every writer employs words, and the manner his manner of thinking; and that, from the peculiarity of thought and expression which belongs to him, there is a certain Character imprinted on his style, which may be denominated his manner; commonly expressed by such general terms, as strong, weak, dry, simple, affected, or the like. These distinctions carry, in general, some reference to an author's manner of thinking, but refer chiefly to his mode of expression. They arise from the whole tenour [tenor] of this language; and comprehend the effect produced by all those parts of Style which we have already considered; the choice which he makes of a single word; his arrangement of these sentences; the degree of his precision; and his embellishment, by means of musical cadence, figures, or other arts of speech, as the result of those underparts of which I have hitherto treated.[6]

Here Blair points toward the underpinnings that support and reinforce the proper use of the structure of language: how it functions; how it is used by communicators, especially in this instance by Taylor. This provides an example of how a preacher uses language as a part of her or his peculiar manner of style. Language structure provides a window into the feeling and thinking soul of a preacher's peculiar manner.

What is more, Blair's insight provides a guidepost for how we want to organize and arrange this chapter. We intend to highlight and identify attributes that are underparts of a peculiar manner, peculiarly attached to a preacher. In this instance, we are focused on the peculiar manner of Gardner Taylor. In this way, we intend to connect the dots between the manner of Taylor, who represents the best of a peculiar manner and style, with that which we consider to be the epitome of manner of thinking "from the peculiarity of thought and expression which belongs to him."[7]

What follows is our effort to present and understand how character is imprinted in style. Further, we seek to underline how those modes of expression, whether weak, strong, or otherwise, communicate volumes about the preacher. This points us toward the link between a preacher and her or his subject that is under consideration.

Finally, we want to address words and word arrangements, which we have alluded to frequently in previous chapters.

We further make plain and clear that Gardner Taylor's pulpit oratory possesses all traditions of rhetoric, but the art of eloquence, which now includes style, remains his predominating tradition. It does not, however, exclude other traditions. Instead, it informs and intersects with the others. Style, we assert, defines the power underneath Taylor's grandeur (what Blair calls ornament and what we have likened to the lovely flowers in a pot). Still, it is Taylor's style that continues to keep listeners on the edge of their seats. To further amplify Taylor's approach, we add what Blair said of style:

> The best definition I can give it is, the peculiar manner in which a man expresses his conceptions, by means of language. It is different from mere Language or words. The words, which an author employs, may be proper and faultless; and his Style may, nevertheless, have great faults; it may be dry, or stiff, or feeble, or affected. Style has always had some reference to an author's manner of thinking. It is a picture of the ideas which rise in his mind, and of the manner in which they rise there; and, hence, when we are examining an author's composition, it is, in many cases, extremely difficult to separate the Style from the sentiment.[8]

Of import here is to reemphasize Blair's claim that style is connected to an author's or preacher's manner of thinking. Furthermore, style, eloquence, and invention point toward the picture of ideas which rise in a preacher's mind. These underparts are identified in a preacher's or author's composition, which throughout our book we refer to as sermonic discourse (Taylor's sermonic discourse follows closely the rules of rhetoric that are present in the work of a novelist). Style and sentiment or eloquence are indeed connected. When preachers learn to connect skillfully the traditions of rhetoric, their sermonic discourses are comprehended as a composed narrative.

This is our focus, and therefore we have written this chapter where we refer to eloquence as style, because together these attributes make too broad a topic for a single chapter. What is more, style too often is mischaracterized and illy associated with pompous sermon delivery. We will address that when we consider what verifiable parts of proper delivery are determined to be in our final chapter. Style then is the manner in which an orator or preacher speaks out—which is uniquely or peculiarly a description of her or his style. Taylor's style "features grand and piercing language, language that wrestles with and grips the hearer."[9] In this manner, we intend to underline that which makes Taylor peculiar and how his style continues to speak out.

Taylor was a master of style. His style informs a preacher's understanding and employment of structures of language and ornamentation in the English tongue. This furthermore helps our understanding of the significance of a single word that leads to phrases that connect sentences to paragraphs. Thus the structure of language is another description of a discourse's organization and arrangement. Of course these words and phrases link and transform sentences into paragraphs. Well-structured paragraphs reinforce our sermonic discourse's original idea that makes persuasive the unconcealed narrative and argument. A well-structured, persuasive argument drives that which lies at the taproot of a narrative.

In addition, we take careful notice of Taylor's use and purposes of word pictures. Here, this is narrowly defined as figurative speech in order to bend and contract or expand interpretation of meaning. Among these rhetorical devices is a proper use of hyperbole: the connective role and power of metaphors and the like. Style is the way an effective preacher links ideas that shape her or his sermonic discourse's argument, which is the pulsing heart of all species of discourse's narrative skeletal formation. We remember that narrative persuades.[10] What persuades is the style of narrative and how it shows that which is underneath the preacher and underlines what informs her or him. In other words, style speaks to a shared pathology—that of the biblical text under consideration, and that of the preacher and the listeners.

How Discourse Surfaces Character

Let us turn to what Blair has referred to as "Eloquence of the Pulpit." This provides a window into how style, character, and the quality of depth surface in a pulpit orator. It is a broad topic, but for our purposes we focus on what Blair expresses to be gravity and warmth. This, we believe, epitomizes the pulpit oratory of Gardner Taylor:

> The chief characteristics of the eloquence suited to the pulpit, as distinguished from the other kinds of public speaking, appear to me to be these two: gravity and warmth. The serious nature of the subjects belonging to the Pulpit requires Gravity; their importance to mankind requires warmth. It is far from being either easy or common to unite these characters of eloquence. The grave, when it is predominant, is apt to run into dull solemnity. The warm, when it wants gravity, borders on the theatrical and light. The union of the two must be studied by all preachers as the utmost consequence, both in the composition of their discourses, and in their manner of delivery. Gravity and warmth united, form that character of preaching the French call Onction [unction or extremes]; the affecting, penetrating, interesting manner, flowing from a strong sensibility of heart in the preacher to the importance of those truths which he delivers, and an earnest desire that they make full impression on the hearts of his hearers.[11]

Blair's words epitomize Taylor's peculiar manner, which is a masterful balance between gravity and warmth. We add that Taylor did not advocate that warmth supersede biblical proclamation. Pulpit oratory demands of preachers to prosecute their surest and most trusted responsibility, which is to proclaim the Word of the Lord. As mentioned previously, Taylor did not support overly simplifying pulpit oratory. He made every attempt to avoid what he called "dumbed down" pulpit oratory. In fact, he insisted that people don't want to be "dumbed down." Instead, Taylor believed people "want to be lifted up."[12] Like Blair, Taylor understood that eloquence joined by the graces of style enhances our pulpit oratory, an art form that informs, amuses, or delights and persuades "in some way or other, to act upon his fellow-creatures."[13]

Character in style is a precise balance between gravity and warmth: between the content and delivery. In addition, it is the dedication to accuracy and an awareness of how listeners will hear the aforementioned. Certainly it adds purpose, for which pulpit oratory exists. It exists to point the weary toward the Trinitarian Godhead. Second, it underscores an imperative, which is that skillful pulpit oratory provides beauty to its content. Third, it surfaces the pulpit orator's character, which highlights too the discourse's character, quality, and depth. Fourth, it focuses listeners upon the pulpit orator's main argument so that it may be examined, understood, enjoyed, and approved. This exemplifies the intersection between the art of eloquence and the art of style. This is at the heart of persuasion.[14] How then do we accomplish style's purposes?

The Structure of Language

We have established firmly that "style is thinking out into language."[15] To perform this necessary task, we now focus our attention on the structure of language. The depth and quality of style then are identified in all species of public speaking, and certainly it is no less identified with pulpit oratory. The latter, however, which is our concern, depends greatly on the character, quality, and depth located in the proper use of words. In short, words matter: how they are organized, how they are arranged, and how they fit together into a discourse. We restate here that "style has always had some reference to an author's manner of thinking. It is a picture of the ideas which rise in his mind, and of the manner in which they rise there."[16] We now make an attempt to simplify the process of the structure of language. We think of this as grammatical competence.

Grammatical competence is the key part of the structure of language.[17] For our purposes, we employ its three major parts: purity, precision, and propriety of word usages. As a whole, these make our pulpit oratory lucid. By this we mean that our oratory should be clear, transparent like glass, clearly expressed, and easily understood. Blair called this Perspicuity: "The study of Perspicuity requires attention, first to single words and phrases and then to the construction of sentences . . . Perspicuity considered with respect to words and phrases requires these three qualities in them: *Purity, Propriety,* and *Precision.*"[18]

We return to "The Strange Ways of God" to highlight how perspicuity, or making the discourse clear, transparent, and glassy, is an employment of the structure of language. First let us define these parts briefly. Purity is an employment of words that construct ideas; these words are not imported from foreign languages. In this instance, we mean that purity of words belong to the idiom of the English language.

Second, propriety in a narrower fashion is selection of such words in the English language. Words that link phrases, sentences, and paragraphs are chosen carefully to establish the best means possible to enable the preacher to express her or his intended thoughts. Third, precision is the most significant aspect and part of perspicuity. A proper use of precision is a guard against faulty expressions of ideas. To be precise then is to say what we mean and no more. This implies that a writer or an orator must be aware that not to be precise may convey images and ideas that she or he does not intend.

The following excerpt from "The Strange Ways of God" is a part of the introduction of Taylor's sermonic discourse. As was previously mentioned, Taylor's introductions are uncommonly protracted. He uses commonplaces effectively and adroitly, and as a result he introduces his sermon thesis masterfully and often nearly unnoticeably. This excerpt (let us call it paragraph 2) immediately follows this sermon's first one that appeared earlier in this chapter:

> For here was a life of such broad grandeur, of such passion and commitment and dedication and discernment and insight that we stand too close to really gauge it. But we do know, though cannot assess it and we cannot establish the true and precise meaning of this life, we know this: that it has affected each of us, and that life has affected this land indelibly and ineradicably. And whatever attempts there may be in this nation to obviate and to obliterate, and whatever neglect or accident of design may be perpetuated against this life, its glow will not go out, and its impact will not lessen, and its force will not dim and will not become vague. How strange![19]

In order to locate the purity of his word choice, we reorganize Taylor's first sentence. At close reading, we notice there are no words foreign to the English language. "We stand too close to really gauge it, for here was a life of such broad grandeur, of such passion and commitment and dedication and discernment and insight." Taylor's style points us toward what we have come to understand to be the structure of language.

This is akin to our clay flower pot's structure and function. In Taylor's second sentence, we locate his thesis: "we know this: that it has affected each of us, and that [his] life has affected this land indelibly and ineradicably." He follows his thesis with a brief argument or justification that is organized, arranged, and properly placed in order to support effectively his thesis: "And whatever attempts there may be in this nation to obviate and to obliterate, and whatever neglect or accident of design may be perpetuated against this life, its glow will not go out, and its impact will not lessen, and its force will not dim and will not become vague."

Earlier, in the first paragraph of "The Strange Ways of God," we highlighted Taylor's word choice. His deliberate word choice forms what we call a thematic pattern: "strange," "shiver," "land," "shadow," and "country." Although Taylor admits that King's life, in 1972, could not be fully understood or appreciated, his thematic pattern forewarns the nation that it cannot ignore King's shadowy presence and impact upon and across the American and global ethical and moral consciousness. This is an example of why we must pay attention closely to language structure and how it links us to ideas.

Language structure then functions as an organization of our words, which is an organization of ideas. Second, Taylor's word choice is an immediate example of what we mean by propriety. Words such as "broad grandeur, such passion, commitment, dedication, discernment and insight" are meant to provide transparent word pictures that convey easily understood ideas. Taylor's word pictures are meant to be understood as metaphoric language and here are used to persuade listeners to imagine the living and breathing King and how he lived nobly.

Taylor then admits that his words will not "establish the true and precise meaning of this life." His word choices are precise so that he may avoid contradicting words expressed by Coretta Scott King: "it will be fifty years before the full assessment of the life of Martin King can begin to be made in this country." As we mentioned, this is a brief definition for how each of these parts functions and how they are quilted together.

In our view, Gardner Taylor's pulpit oratory epitomizes these major parts: purity, propriety, and precision. The parts help us get underneath Taylor's art of style. In our opening epigraph, we set our global positioning system (GPS) toward this point, in order to reinforce our claim. That is, what remains our goal is located in that which Taylor once wrote: "I urge all preachers to take a single word most seriously . . . I think that we need to recover a sense of preaching as an art form, one that features grand and piercing language, language that wrestles with and grips the hearer."[20]

This underlines our attempt to get beneath the flowers and the potted dirt. It helps us to get beneath where the flowers' roots deeply grow undisturbed. We too get beneath the potter's clay flower pot; we recall that it is adorned with beautiful fault lines that add character to its composition, which links us to the pot's narrative. In this way, we are able to understand that the flowers' roots reach deeply and naturally into the soil in order to grow in form and beauty. Once more, we see the beauty and function of the potter's clay flower pot, and we see a connection between the pot and discourse. In short, we see style: "Style cannot be proper without being also pure; and where both purity and propriety meet, besides making style perspicuous [clear], they also render it graceful."[21] Thus, we see a linking connection between ornamentation and structure.

Ornamentation and Structure

Imagine that Taylor is the potter and his style is the clay flower pot or the structure of language and the flowers or ornamentation. Let us rename the pot to be a clear and transparent language, which is perspicuity. Its function is to enable the potted flowers' roots to reach deeply and grow naturally. The flowers then are beauty, which is ornamentation. His clay pot then is the structure of language. Blair describes this as parts of style:

> All qualities of a good style may be ranged under two heads, perspicuity and ornament. For all that can possibly be required of language, is, to convey our ideas to the minds of others, and, at the same time, in such dress, as by pleasing and interesting them, shall most effectually strengthen the impressions which we seek to make. When both these ends are answered, we certainly accomplish every purpose for which we use writing and discourse.[22]

For a final example of how Taylor's structure of language and ornamentation function in an oral discourse, let us return to Taylor's "The Strange Ways of God." We will characterize the following excerpts as paragraphs 3–4. When referring to this sermon discourse's paragraph 3, Richard Lischer comments that "on one occasion as he [Taylor] read some of the proper names in Luke 3 (Tiberius, Ituraea, Trachonitis), members of the congregation began responding, "My Lord, my Lord!"[23] This is significant in large part because in paragraph 4, Taylor is not reading Luke 3:1-2 but in fact is reciting it from memory. What is repetition and cadence, Blair calls a "musical cadence."[24] In addition, in paragraph 4, we will focus on Taylor's employment of word choices that strengthen his sentence structures (purity, propriety, and precision of language). What is noticed is how Taylor's mastery of word structure and ornamentation helps shape his persuasive narrative.

How strange!

What is the clue to this? God comes at us in strange ways and from such unexpected and, to many of us, apparently awkward angles. What is the clue to this? Well, let me cite another example which may help to set this in its proper context. That is this word recorded in the Gospel of Luke: "In the fifteenth year of the reign of Tiberius Caesar, Pontius Pilate being governor of Judea, and Herod being tetrarch of Galilee, and his brother Philip tetrarch of Ituraea and of the region of Trachonitis, Lysanias the tetrarch of Abilene, Annas and Caiaphas being the high priests, the word of God came unto John the son of Zacharias in the wilderness" (Luke 3:1-2).

When you start calling these names, it sounds like a roll call of the people who really mattered and on whose side the future lay and to whom the coming generations belonged. Tiberius Caesar, and one thinks of purple and high-ceilinged palaces. Courtiers, screaming eagles of the legions, standing sentinels at the farthest outposts of empire, at the very extreme borders which civilized men counted it worthy to rule. Tiberius Caesar, successor to Augustus, with the Forum in Rome there at one end and over the Coliseum. All roads leading to and from Rome with its seven hills of imperial glory. "In the fifteenth year of the reign of Tiberius Caesar, Pontius Pilate being governor of Judea"— and one thinks of the second line of command, prouder usually in the colonies than even at home, the representation of all the grandeur and glory of Rome, "Pontius Pilate being governor of Judea, and Herod being tetrarch of Galilee,"—the splendor of the court of an oriental monarch—"Annas and Caiaphas. . . " Annas, banished in the intricacies and turbulence of Judean politics from his own place as high

priest, but having had the resourcefulness and shrewdness to introduce his son-in-law, Joseph Caiaphas, as chief high priest. The glory of
ecclesiastical authority, "Annas and Caiaphas being the high priests,"
and you begin to think all that can be said about where power was
and where influence lay had already been uttered. "In the fifteenth
year of the reign of Tiberius Caesar, Pontius Pilate being governor of
Judea, and Herod being tetrarch of Galilee . . . Annas and Caiaphas
being the high priests"—and what is really happening is that the man
is establishing some background and setting the stage and describing
the scenery for something really important. "In the fifteenth year of
the reign of Tiberius Caesar, Pontius Pilate being governor of Judea,
and Herod being tetrarch of Galilee, . . . Annas and Caiaphas being the
high priests, the word of God came to John . . . in the wilderness."[25]

In paragraph 3, Taylor twice said, ""What is the clue to this?"
This is a brilliant way to alert his congregation that he's transitioning
from his introduction's commonplaces ornamentation to the body of
his thesis and argument. When referring to his thesis, "We know this:
that it [the life of Martin King] has affected each of us, and that life
has affected this land indelibly and ineradicably," Taylor reinforces
it with a short rephrase of his previous argument, "God comes at
us in strange ways and from such unexpected and, to many of us,
apparently awkward angles." This is to reinforce the significance of
King's life. He then reads the passage, which is Luke 3:1-2, and his
congregation responds with "My Lord, my Lord!"

Taylor begins paragraph 4 with "When you start calling these
names, it sounds like a roll call of people who really mattered." Taylor is smart here, because he anticipates his congregation's approval
of his oral reading. Under most circumstances, publically, it is difficult to correctly pronounce these uncommon words. This is the art of
eloquence, and Taylor is its master. In order to develop the important
political relationships of the characters in the passage, Taylor repeats
"Tiberius Caesar" five times, "Pontius Pilate" four times, "Herod
being tetrarch of Galilee" three times, "Annas and Caiaphas" in a
couplet four times, and "In the fifteenth year of the reign of Tiberius
Caesar" three times. As a significant part of his rhetorical strategy,
Taylor uses these words to create and shape the contours and boundaries of his narrative's development.

Taylor's narrative then has guideposts (which denote distance traveled) that move from Rome's "high-ceilinged palaces" to "the farthest outposts of empire, at the very extreme borders which civilized men counted it worthy to rule." In each instance, Taylor chooses careful words that are pure, of propriety, and precise. His words are not foreign to the English language. He is careful not to introduce words that are outside the immediate comprehension of his congregation. His words are organized and arranged carefully to build into sentences that are appropriate to create word pictures. His words are precise to express what he means and no more. Words such as "purple and high-ceilinged palaces," "courtiers," "screaming eagles of the legions," "seven hills of imperial glory," "grandeur and glory of Rome," "the splendor of the court of an oriental monarch," and "the glory of ecclesiastical authority" are examples that demonstrate Taylor's understanding of the structure of language and ornament.

Robert William Dale, Joseph Parker, Charles Haddon Spurgeon, Leslie Dixon Weatherhead, and the eminent Alexander Maclaren were nineteenth-century British Victorian pulpit luminaries. Like these luminaries, Gardner Taylor is our twentieth century's master of Victorian eloquence. Taylor was committed deeply to black Victorianism; however, he did not preach the gospel from the same social location as the British luminaries. That is, Taylor did not occupy a position akin to that of the sociocultural predominating culture's class distinction that was reinforced by racial privilege.

This is a primary reason that we asserted why Taylor's image has been chiseled onto the Mount Rushmore of preachers of African American descent. These are preachers who interpret Scripture and the world through a sociomarginalized lens. They remain informants for current guardians of the oppressed and those who live within the veil. Throughout the twentieth century's cultural upheavals and racial hostilities, Gardner Taylor eloquently and prophetically preached into that chaos and vacuum.

This is significant and provides an appropriate context for Taylor's preaching abilities and his rhetorical aims. It is only when we examine what is underneath the ornamentation that we discover an authentic essence of his peculiar manner and his pulpit oratory. There is no single reason for his peculiar manner, but it does demand that we revise the twentieth century's historical and political impediments that he faced in his pursuit toward achieving human justice. This is his experience, and it precisely lies at the taproot of Taylor's peculiar manner. His eloquence or ornamentation then is informed by what is underneath the surface.

Conclusion

A careful examination of the clay flower pot with its fault lines, and the flowers and their roots that grow deeply into the dirt, serves as an informant into Taylor's manner of thinking out loud—which is style. Into Taylor's art of style, we have a window. Taylor's sermonic discourse, "The Strange Ways of God," would not have been so effective and affecting without our understanding that Taylor knew King and shared his passions, ambitions, and hope for the world's future.

We began this chapter with our definition of a peculiar manner, which is a manner of style, and how it applies to Taylor's preaching prowess. We suggested that a peculiar manner best describes the art of style which is peculiar to Gardner Taylor. By using the metaphor of the clay flower pot with fault lines and potted flowers with deep roots, we focused our attention on creating a word picture to help us define the art of style. In chapter 5, we will examine Taylor's art of memory and narrowly focus our attention on critical memory and how that helps us link the art of memory to the previously examined traditions of rhetoric.

Epigraph

G. Avery Lee and Gardner C. Taylor, *Perfecting the Pastor's Art: Wisdom from Avery Lee and Gardner Taylor* (Valley Forge, PA: Judson Press, 1995), 43.

NOTES

1. Gardner C. Taylor, "The Strange Ways of God," in *Essential Taylor*, disc 2, vol. 4 (Valley Forge, PA: Judson Press, 2000). This audio sermon recording is gripping and touches human emotions viscerally.

2. Gardner C. Taylor, "The Strange Ways of God," in *The Words of Gardner Taylor*, comp. Edward Taylor, vol. 4: *Special Occasions and Expository Sermons* (Valley Forge, PA: Judson Press, 2001), 100.

3. Ibid.

4. Ibid.

5. Hugh Blair, *Lectures on Rhetoric and Belles Lettres*, ed. Linda Ferreira-Buckley and S. Michael Halloran, Landmarks in Rhetoric and Public Address (1783; Carbondale: Southern Illinois University Press, 2005), 197.

6. Ibid.

7. Ibid.

8. Ibid., 99.

9. G. Avery Lee and Gardner C. Taylor, *Perfecting the Pastor's Art: Wisdom from Avery Lee and Gardner Taylor* (Valley Forge, PA: Judson Press, 1995), 43.

10. Jacqueline Bacon, *The Humblest May Stand Forth: Rhetoric, Empowerment, and Abolition* (Columbia: University of South Carolina Press, 2002), 60–61.

11. Blair, *Lectures on Rhetoric and Belles Lettres*, 318.

12. Lee and Taylor, *Perfecting the Pastor's Art*, 43.

13. Ibid.

14. Hugh Blair, "Eloquence or Public Speaking—History of Eloquence—Grecian Eloquence—Demosthenes," in *Lectures on Rhetoric and Belles Lettres*, ed. Linda Ferreira-Buckley and S. Michael Halloran, Landmarks in Rhetoric and Public Address (1783; Carbondale: University of Southern Illinois, 2005), 264–65. There are some who write on these matters and believe that a larger distinction can be made between eloquence and style. We cannot; these are nearly inseparable and should be explained simultaneously. Still, that has been proven to be difficult even for the most skillful homileticians and rhetoricians. Because this is true, we have decided to provide a fuller context, that is, how eloquence and style intersect. We keep in mind that style has more to say about what is underneath the oratory which surfaces and reveals the character and quality of depth of the pulpit orator. Nevertheless, we believe that revisiting eloquence in this chapter on style helps us to see why two chapters are necessary to demonstrate that eloquence and style are verifiably connected.

Of eloquence, in particular, it is the more necessary to ascertain the proper notion, because there is not anything concerning which false notion have been more prevalent. Hence, it has been so often, and is still at this day, in disrepute with many. When you speak to a plain man of eloquence [we remind readers that style is connected here], or in praise of it, he is apt to hear you with very little attention. He conceives Eloquence to signify a certain trick of speech; the art of vanishing weak arguments plausibility; or of speaking so as to please and tickle the ear. "Give me good sense," says he, "and keep your eloquence for boys." He is in the right, if Eloquence were what he conceives it to be. It would be then a very contemptible art indeed, below the study of any wise or good man. But nothing can be more remote from truth. To be truly eloquent, is to speak with a purpose. For the best definition which, I think, can be given of eloquence is the art of speaking in such a manner as to attain the end for which we speak. Whenever a man speaks or writes, he is supposed, as a rational being, to have some end in view; either to inform, or to amuse, or to persuade, or in such manner as to adapt all his words most effectually to that end, is the most eloquent man. Whatever the subject be, there is room for eloquence; in history or even philosophy, as well as in orations. The definition which I have of eloquence, comprehends all the different kinds of it; whether calculated to instruct, to persuade, or to please. But, as the most important subject of discourse is action, or conduct, the power of eloquence chiefly appears when it is employed to influence conduct, and persuade to action. As it is principally with reference to this end, that it becomes the object of art, eloquence may, under this view of it, be defined, the art of persuasion.

This being once established, certain consequences immediately follow, which point out the fundamental maximums of the art. It follows clearly, that in order to persuade, the most essential requisites are, solid argument, clear method, a character of probity appearing in the Speaker, joined with such graces of style and utterance, as shall draw our attention to what he says. Good sense is the foundation of all. No man can be truly eloquent without it, for fools can persuade none but fools. In order to persuade a man of sense, you must first convince him; which is only done, by satisfying his understanding of the reasonableness of what you propose to him.

15. Edward P. J. Corbett and Robert J. Connors, "Style," in *Classical Rhetoric for the Modern Student*, 4th ed. (Oxford: Oxford University Press, 1999), 337.

16. Blair, *Lectures on Rhetoric and Belles Lettres*, 99.

17. Ibid., 110–11. Blair provides essential notes for those who take seriously grammatical construction of sentences, how they function and struc-

ture larger ideas, especially through illustrations or what we call consistently in our book's main text word pictures, which is another way to express metaphoric or figurative language:

> Having begun to treat of Style, in the last lecture I considered in fundamental quality, perspicuity. What I have said of this, relates chiefly to the choice of words. From words, I proceed to sentences; and as, in all writing and discourse, the proper composition and structure of sentences is of the highest importance, [and] I shall treat of this fully. Though perspicuity be the general head under which I, at present, consider language, I shall not confine myself to this quality alone, in sentences, but shall enquire also, what is requisite grace and beauty: that I may bring together all that seems necessary to be attended to in the construction and arrangement of words in a Sentence.
>
> The first variety that occurs in the consideration of sentences, is, the distinction of long and short ones. The precise length of sentences, as to the number of words, or the number of members, which may enter into them, cannot be ascertained by any definite measure. At the same time, it is obvious; there may be an extreme on either side. Sentences, immoderately long, and consisting of too many members, always transgress some one or other of the rules which I shall mention soon, as necessary to be observed in every good sentence. In discourses that are to be spoken, regard must be had to the easiness of pronunciation, which is not consistent with too long periods. In compositions where pronunciation has no place, still, however, by using long periods too frequently, an author overloads the reader's ear, and fatigues his attention. For long periods require evidently, more attention than short ones, in order to perceive clearly the connection of the several parts, and to take the whole at one view. At the same time, there may be an excess in too many short sentences also; by which the sense is split and broken, the connection of thought weakened, and the memory burdened, by presenting to it a long succession of minute objects.

18. Ibid., 100–1. Blair writes,

Purity and propriety of language, are often used indiscriminately for each other; and, indeed, they are very nearly allied. A distinction, however, obtains between them. Purity, is the use of such words, and such constructions, as belong to the idiom of the language which we speak; in opposition to words and phrases that are imported from other Languages, or that are obsolete, or new-coined, or used without proper authority. Propriety, is the selection of such words in the language, as the best and the most established usage has appointed to those ideas which we intend to express by them. It implies the correct and happy application of them according to that usage, in opposition to vulgarisms, or low expressions; and to words and phrases, which would be less significant of the ideas what we mean to convey. Style may be pure, that is, it may all be strictly English, without Scottisms, or Gallicisms, or ungrammatical irregular expressions of any kind, and may, nevertheless, be deficient in propriety. The words may be ill chosen; not adapted to the subject, nor fully expressive of the author's sense. He has taken all his words and phrases from the general mass of English language; but he has made his selection among these words unhappily.

19. Taylor, "Strange Ways of God," 100–101.

20. Lee and Taylor, *Perfecting the Pastor's Art*, 43.

21. Blair, *Lectures on Rhetoric and Belles Lettres*, 101.

22. Ibid., 100.

23. Richard Lischer, *The Preacher King: Martin Luther King Jr. and the Word That Moved America* (Oxford: Oxford University Press, 1995), 41.

24. Blair, *Lectures on Rhetoric and Belles Lettres*, 197.

25. Taylor, "Strange Ways of God," 101–2.

5

"Blessed with a Good Memory"
The Art of Memory

The fourth part of rhetoric was memoria . . . concerned with memorizing speeches. Of all the five parts of rhetoric, memoria was the one that received the least attention in the rhetoric books. The reason for the neglect of this aspect of rhetoric is probably that not much can be said, in a theoretical way, about the process of memorizing; and after rhetoric came to be concerned mainly with written discourse, there was no further need to deal with memorizing. —Edward P. J. Corbett and Robert J. Connors

I've been blessed with a good memory. Even the impressions of earliest childhood remain vivid. —Gardner C. Taylor

We begin with four important admissions. First, the art of memory as it is defined conventionally is the art of mastering memorization skills. This art and skill is mastered by only a few orators and preachers. Second, we contend that Gardner Taylor is among them. Third, although it takes time, disciplined study, and determination, the art of memory can be learned. Fourth, the art of memory in our view is not solely a mastery of memorization skills. As you will see, the art of memory is better understood as a way to help listeners remember a preacher's sermon content.

Therefore, we will focus our efforts on presenting a theory that we suggest will help us to remember a sermon's content. The art of memory properly deployed means that people remember the content of the sermon. We contend that a sermon shaped with the use of a narrative is a preacher's best approach for the audience to remember its content. The art of memory then is such skills and tactics that persuade audiences. Expressed another way, the art of memory's tactics and skill are located in a preacher's ethos, logos, and pathos. First, the preacher's ethos, that is, her or his character, provides to the preacher a sense of credibility with her or his audiences. "In rhetoric we commonly find ethos in the sense of a good disposition or habit of choice. The ethos of the speaker as shown in his speech ought to be good, for the audience will not trust a speaker if they think him bad."[1]

When an audience respects the preacher's commitment to his or her craft, it listens differently. In comparison, when an audience does not respect the preacher's commitment to the craft, also it listens differently. Whether listeners make conscious or subconscious decisions, nonetheless listeners critique or judge the credibility, or ethos, of the preachers.

Second, we assert that a preacher's logos, that is, her or his ability to make a plausible argument, is a factor. A plausible argument adds to a preacher's credibility. This is form over function, but it does matter. An audience appreciates how a preacher's argument is arranged, organized, and delivered with an intention that the audience understands and considers the claims made. Here we provide a definition for logos:

> [P]ersuasion is effected by the arguments, when we demonstrate the truth, real or apparent, by such means as inhere in particular cases. [This] calls for a man who can logically, analyze the types of human character, along with virtues, and, thirdly, can analyze the emotions— the nature and quality of each several emotion, with means by which, and the manner in which it is excited.[2]

A preacher's proper use of arrangement and organization is a skill and tactic to persuade. Furthermore, we take notice that preachers craft their arguments with their audience in mind—we take notice of the types of character, virtues, and emotions that function in every audience. Our goal is that our arguments are remembered.

And third, we emphasize that a preacher's pathos, that is, her or his ability to create a sympathetic narrative, is of utmost importance. An audience is more likely to remember what they have been told when the message is emotionally attractive; that is, an audience may feel it necessary to support the preacher in her or his pilgrimage or campaign and decide to make it their own. Indeed, they remember it. "[P]ersuasion is effected through the audience when they are brought by the speech into a state of emotion [pathos]; for we give very different decisions under sway of pain or joy, and liking or hatred. This we contend, is the sole aspect of the art with which technical writers of the day have tried to deal."[3]

The sympathetic, which is pathos, must be carefully deployed by a preacher. We must avoid any perception that we intend to exploit people with empty emotional platitudes and crescendos. Rather, we intend that people appreciate our honest attachment to our arguments made. In this way, we hope that people will remember our arguments and attach themselves alongside. Ethos, logos, and pathos are skills and tactics to help preachers create an intersection between the art of memory and narrative. If the preacher is credible, and the argument is plausible, and the preacher gains emotional attachment and trust to the narrative, then the narrative is persuasive.

Beyond Memorization: Crafting a Persuasive Narrative

Taylor possessed, understood, and deployed these skills tactically in order to accomplish his rhetorical goals. We keep in mind that he was capable of organizing and arranging his mental images into ideas and deploying them into verbal actions. This process scholars and scientists call the mental mapping process. By this, we mean the ability to mentally arrange and organize what is on the inside and verbally express imaginative actions on the outside:

> Human behavior has both a cognitive side [mental mapping]—the understanding of situations—and an active side [verbal actions]—the

operation of the person on the situation. . . . The cognitive side of language is in its grammar—its system for defining the situation. The operative side is in its use of language to effect the situation—its rhetoric. "Grammar" and "rhetoric" are key terms.[4]

In short, this is an ability that is endowed to some. This ability helps endowed orators and preachers to understand human behavior. We associate human behavior with mental organization, arrangement, and verbal actions. We call this nexus the ability to create word pictures, an integral part of narrative development, and at times it can double as artifice and ornament.[5] We have located this ability in the works of Gardner Taylor, who was "blessed with a good memory." This serves as a segue to our analysis of the fourth tradition of rhetoric.

We admit here that the fourth tradition of rhetoric is the least written about and the least understood. This is precisely because the art of memory is a process of mental arrangements, organization, and verbal actions. It is of import to state there are ongoing psychological and neurological studies that have enhanced our understanding of mental mapping and verbal actions that occur between the mind and the brain that were not available to ancient rhetorical theorists.

According to Barbara Tversky, "It's almost impossible to separate mind and brain. They are connected through behavior; it's by looking at the brain as organisms behave that we are able to infer the neural substrates."[6] (Neural substrates are an integral part of the central nervous system, which controls behavior.) These scientific and psychological explanations became widely known after many of the ancient rhetorical treatises were developed and written. Without an awareness of these psychological and neurological breakthroughs, the ancient listeners' rhetorical cultural expectations were to witness their orators' mastery of memorization on full display.

Memorization skills then were reinforced by the ancients' formation of schools that trained orators to memorize their public addresses. These schools, however, are not different from some of our schools' schemes are today. We have all seen overpromising advertisements, the kinds that make difficult learned behaviors seem simple to master in a brief amount of time. This serves as an example of such an advertisement: "I Can Give You a Retentive Memory in

Thirty Days."[7] We do not intend to oversimplify the art of memory as we define it. Preachers must doggedly study and pursue a level of comfort and competence in the art. However, it can be learned.

In addition to ancient orators not having access to psychological and neurological breakthroughs, neither did they have access to contemporary modern technologies such as Teleprompters, PowerPoint™ presentations, and other print and electronic communication gadgets. Thus, it was necessary for orators to memorize the content of their public addresses (and practice their oratorical delivery, as you will see in the next chapter). Many who heard orators who possessed effective memorization skills were persuaded by the orator's arguments. Of course, this is the ultimate goal for an effective address. In addition, to see a person prosecute a public address without notes added artifice and ornament to an address. When it is done appropriately, it continues to add artifice and ornament to our contemporary addresses.

In short, artifice and ornamentation were the stock-and-trade tools used by most orators. We emphasize here that nineteenth-century orators understood that their public addresses were not judged by their substantive content alone. Their addresses were judged by their entertainment value also. Nineteenth-century audiences anticipated and expected to hear long and dramatic addresses. These addresses were recited from memory, similar to their forebears, the ancient orators. Lincoln's Gettysburg Address is a rare exception to that general rule. These excerpts underscore the culture and context for which the Gettysburg Address took place:

> The normal purgative for such occasions was a large-scale solemn act of oratory, a kind of performance art with great power over audiences in the middle of the nineteenth century.
>
> Some later accounts would emphasize the length of the main speech at the Gettysburg dedication, as if that were an ordeal or an imposition on the audience. But a talk of several hours was customary and expected then—much like the length and pacing of a modern rock concert. The crowds that heard Lincoln debate Stephen Douglas in 1858, through three-hour engagements, were delighted to hear Daniel Webster and other orators of the day recite composed paragraphs that filled two hours at the least.[8]

The champion at such declamatory occasions, after the death of Webster, was Webster's friend Edward Everett. Everett was that rare being, a scholar and Ivy League diplomat who could hold mass audiences in thrall. His voice, diction, and gestures were dramatic, and he always performed his carefully written text, no matter how long, from memory.[9] His speech at Gettysburg "was like a modern day 'docudrama' on television, telling the story of the recent events on the basis of investigative reporting."[10]

Everett was considered the most skillful orator of this time, capable of prosecuting this species of public address that befitted the occasion. We point toward Everett's possession of the art of memory as an example of the conventional definition that we have described in the opening paragraph of this chapter. His public addresses are a point of departure worthy of study for contemporary preachers who make an attempt to craft intersections between the art of memory and narrative. We take notice that Everett crafted his narratives similar to how a local or cable news television anchor prepares her script: she prepares it as one part news and the other part as entertainment.

Everett's rhetoric mirrors expectations and the cultural climate from which it grew. It grew from that which is similar to the ancient orator's orations. "The orator's memory was trained largely through constant practice (just as professional actors today acquire an amazing facility in memorizing a script), but the rhetors did suggest various mnemonic devices that facilitated the memorizing of speeches."[11] We shall see that like Everett, other nineteenth-century orators, namely, Abraham Lincoln and Frederick Douglass, were informed by their study of classical rhetorical traditions (and in Douglass's case, *The Columbian Orator*).[12]

Recently, however, theorists have suggested that it is no longer necessary to memorize a speech or a sermon in order to persuade our contemporary audiences. That has changed in part because we have the advantage of advanced technologies that were not available to ancient orators. What is more, this is plausible to accept in our highly advanced technological twenty-first century. We have all witnessed nearly every public official use these technical aids. In many circles, the art of memorization is not a necessary expectation. Memorization is less important now for delivering a successful and effective sermon or speech.

In fact, we can write and deliver our sermons with the same punctiliar detail and attention as a novelist or a screenwriter does for her or his novel or film. Therefore, we assert that the art of memory is better understood as a function of linking ideas through word pictures (mental mapping). In short, we reimagine that the art of memory is an effective function that facilitates for writers and orators an effective tool for developing an effective narrative. An effective narrative leads to an effective sermon.

Theoretically, narratives have characters, settings, and plotlines.[13] These parts help to move the narrative's action toward its significance and meaning. Here, we highlight that an effective narrative is persuasive when it gives its characters voice. "When the narrator-storyteller is effective, it is because she or he has been persuasive in telling their story. It is the narrator-storyteller's ability [and training] that gives voice to the characters."[14] Also, an effective narrative gives voice to the voiceless (a narrative that is crafted through sociomarginalized writers' and orators' voice or voices).

In *Killing Rage: Ending Racism*, bell hooks impassionedly makes this case. Notice how she makes her audience aware that women of African descent and of color are not included in defining the existential threat which remains hegemonic constructs of race, economics, politics, and gender:

> When I first left the apartheid South, to attend a predominately white institution of higher education, I was not in touch with my rage. I had been raised to dream only of racial uplift, of a day when white and black would live together as one. I had been raised to turn the other cheek. However, the fresh air of white liberalism encountered when I went to the West Coast to attend college in the early seventies invited me to let go some of the terror and mistrust of white people living in apartheid had bred in me. The terror keeps all rage at bay. I remember my first feelings of political rage against racism. They surfaced within me after I had read [Franz] Fanon, [Albert] Memmi, [Paulo] Freire. They came as I was reading Malcolm X's autobiography. As Cornel West suggests in his essay, I felt that Malcolm X dared black folks to

claim our emotional subjectivity and that we could do this only by claiming our rage.[15]

hooks creates a narrative that underlines her memory of her personal trauma that shaped and caused her rage. In the preceding excerpt, hooks is her narrative's main character. And "the apartheid South," which she cast as her narrative's main setting, serves as a frame of reference. At close reading, hooks provides her audience with a window into her worldview. hooks describes sociopsychological subjugation and how this subjugation demeans human life. This is effective because it is piercingly descriptive. In addition, we see an intersection between narrative and the art of memory.

As she tells her story, we can feel segregation's grip on her body and segregation's grasp over her mind. What hooks describes is nothing less than immoral dehumanization. We can feel her justified rage. Her intellectual and emotional awakings happened in a distant land (the West Coast at a predominately Anglo institution). Ironically, it is there that she reads broadly about herself (Fanon, Memmi, Freire, and Alex Haley's Malcolm X). The well-known literary names are proponents of pan-Africanism and human justice, a cause that hooks continues to advocate. This intersection of her characters also frames her narrative's minor plotline. The minor plotline has minor characters, which includes well-known, prophetic Cornel West. Of import, the narrative is meant to explain her justified rage. This narrative is persuasive and effective and a brilliant use of memory. hooks weaves her childhood and how it shaped her rage and how it informs her advocacy for human justice.

hooks's narrative is an example of how writers and orators can shape their narrative plot. What is more, hooks demonstrates how mental actions become mental mapping. She has arranged and organized what is on the inside and made it illustrative on the outside. She has demonstrated how to employ word pictures, and in this instance, she places geographical mental markers into her narrative so that readers are oriented to her distance traveled from the American South to the American West. She adroitly implies that there are cultural differences between the West Coast and her native American South. For hooks, the West Coast represents cultural freedom, advancement, and liberation. This is an effective example for how to craft an effective narrative.

An effective narrative then is enhanced with an effective use of word pictures. In this instance, hooks employs word pictures to demonstrate a proper use of an intersection that exists between past and current events, which is the art of memory and narrative. Her mental mapping expressed on the outside as word pictures plays a central role in making her narrative's claims attractive and appealing. Thus, we suggest that the art of memory continues to be important to preachers and the like, but a contemporary preacher's understanding of the art of memory is enhanced when we reimagine its role in effective communication. Memory is significant when preachers and others properly understand that the function and role of the art of memory in the twenty-first century is linking concepts and ideas, which is an integral part of building an effective narrative. We reinforce here that an effective, remembered narrative leads to an effective sermon, a remembered sermon.

George Kennedy, a consequential rhetorician, has thought about the import of the art of memory. That is, the art of memory has a significant role to play in narrative development. Kennedy makes clear that when narrative formation includes familiar settings, that is, settings that can trigger a kind of tablet in the mind and include word pictures, symbols, and social contexts, these are a large representation of the memorization processes.

> A background is a physical setting, familiar to the student, and can be thought of as a tablet in the mind. Against this background the student imagines pictures that symbolize the ideas or the words of a speech in the order in which they should occur. When the student is speaking, this picture is then passed in review in the mind to suggest the thoughts or words. The system works, and still has some use today, but is cumbersome in memorizing a long text, and is probably most useful in exercising the memory to point where it can gain an unaided ability to remember a composition, or as a way of remembering some particular difficult passage verbatim. Ancient orators sometimes used notes, but the reading of a speech from a written text was considered ineffective in political or legal contexts and usually avoided. There are many ancient testimonies to the great potential of the human mind to

remember material verbatim in a society that was far more oral than ours and put high value on such ability.[16]

Kennedy has written extensively on the subject of rhetoric and its traditions. In fact, Kennedy reports that the art of memory can be traced to the fifth century BC. Over a course of time, memorization became a separate function; however, less attention was given to the art in some rhetorical handbooks. What follows, we find significant. Kennedy suggests that rhetoric students were taught to associate word memorization with a particular setting, which we have characterized as word pictures.

In an earlier chapter, we mentioned that Gardner Taylor possessed and mastered the art of invention. With this in mind we can add it to the process of mental mapping. It takes invention in order to marshal an intersection between the art of memory and narrative which is located in word pictures. These are integral parts of shaping a masterful narrative. We have located our intersection between the art of memory and narrative in Taylor's sermon structure, which he calls a sermon journey:

> I think of a sermon as a journey, a trip I want to make. I want to know where I'm starting, how to get there, and where I hope to end up. Incidentally, for preachers who want to work without manuscripts in the pulpit and who have trouble memorizing their sermon, this idea of a journey is very helpful; if you get a sense of progression in your sermon you have a large part of the battle won.[17]

What Taylor describes is aligned closely with our proposition. Namely, we understand that the art of memory and its intersection with narrative is an effective way to develop a gripping sermon discourse. We contend that like hooks, Taylor employed word pictures as markers (mental mapping). These rhetorical tools kept him on his charted course, and at the same time Taylor was able to adroitly keep his audience on the same course with him. As preachers, we too can chart our sermonic journey toward our specific sermon goals. Sermonic discourse then is a progressive journey, and our discourse can improve markedly by deliberately placing word pictures in our sermons as strategic junctures.

Charting a Journey Toward Sermon Goals

How these strategic junctures function were on display in an iconic Gardner Taylor sermon that was preached at Washington, DC's Metropolitan African Methodist Episcopal Church. The date was January 20, 1993. The occasion was an inaugural worship service for then president-elect William Jefferson Clinton. We shall focus on how Taylor masterfully uses an intersection between the art of memory and narrative. Although we shall include three major movements in the sermon, first we focus on Taylor's art of memory. What is more, we shall take note of how Taylor's art of memory served a dual purpose.

Taylor was brilliant at arranging and organizing his sermon content. He carefully uses words such as those we have located in his inauguration sermon's introduction which he uses to connect ideas of life, death, rebirth, and the meaning of life to his magnum opus recital, which is a recital of parts of the United States Declaration of Independence. Second, we shall take notice where Taylor positions his recitals in order to reset the national collective consciousness around what Taylor determines to be the nation's social needs. This is a brilliant example of the intersection between the art of memory and narrative.

The worship service began with Gardner Taylor seated on the pulpit platform of the Metropolitan Church. The pews were filled with Washington insiders and other politicos. When he stood, all would have observed his stately decorum; he was dressed in his familiar black robe widely gapped and flowing open. All would have seen the three black chevrons embroidered into each sleeve and peeking through; all would have detected his white shirt, black tie, and his black-suit vest. Often, we see Oxford and Cambridge academics dressed similarly during public ceremonies.

By then Taylor was known well as a master of the art of eloquence. Already he had appeared in large, small, and prominent pulpits throughout the world. At the same time, he had lectured on homiletics in most of America's and Europe's most prestigious universities, colleges, and seminaries. His stately presence could cause some to mistake his professional identity. Taylor's physical bearing was similar to that of a barrister, a university professor, or a college or seminary president. Some may have compared Taylor's physical bearing with that of a political statesman. Taylor was a polished man. He was someone we can imagine standing in the well of the United States Senate or someone standing on the floor of the House of Commons in Great Britain, where all would listen to him persuasively argue against human injustice and tyranny.

More than a statesman, Taylor was one of the twentieth century's most famous preachers of the English-speaking world. As previously mentioned, on January 20, 1993, the seventy-six-year-old Gardner Taylor would preach a civic sermon that would affirm his prominent place in American history. Seated before him were president-elect William Jefferson Clinton, vice president-elect Albert Arnold Gore Jr., and their families. Other luminaries present were Ronald Harmon Brown and Alexis Margaret Herman, who would become Clinton's Commerce Secretary and Labor Secretary respectively; Reverend Doctor Otis Moss Jr., a prominent Baptist pulpiteer; and Reverend Jesse Louis Jackson Sr., once one of Dr. Martin Luther King Jr.'s civil rights lieutenants and an eventual United States presidential candidate.

On this occasion, Taylor preached "Facing Facts with Faith" (Luke 10:25-28). We characterize his discourse as a civic sermon.[18] A civic sermon intersects religious ideals and symbols with those similar to the democratic tradition. Often, Taylor's sermon introductions are protracted, but Taylor uses his introductions adroitly to state his sermon thesis.

> Across the broad face of this land there is a sense today, and beyond this land, I am sure, of a new energy and vigor being turned loose affirmatively in the coming to incumbency of our new president and vice president. It is as if we have come again to Camelot, but this time with the atmosphere of the Ozarks and in the accents of the great Southern American heartland, and we rejoice in that meeting. A lawyer meets a savior.[19]

> This parable Jesus relates at this meeting has come to be called the parable of the good Samaritan. How strange that an itinerate preacher without possessions in a third-rate province of what looked like a

beaten path of history, in one of the backwaters of the empire, should have told a story, and the title for it has passed into the verbiage of two millennia. How strange, unless he was something more than human.[20]

A lawyer, appropriately enough, asked the question, and I take it that that craft is not underrepresented here today, "What shall I do to inherit eternal life?" Whether capriciously or sincerely, this lawyer had touched the raw nerve of our human existence. Why are we here? What is our purpose? We come out of darkness into this lighted room. . . . What is the significance of it? What is the meaning of the high hope that lifts in our hearts and the dreams that people our days and the sense of purpose? What does it all mean?[21]

Taylor paints a word picture to describe global interest in the election of William Jefferson Clinton: "Across the broad face of this land there is a sense today, and beyond this land, I am sure, of a new energy and vigor being turned loose affirmatively in the coming to incumbency of our new president."

He describes metaphorically Clinton's incumbency to a rebirth of the nation's democratic ideals. In addition, he compares this rebirth with Camelot, another metaphor that is a part of the folklore of the presidency of a youthful John F. Kennedy (1917–1963). Also, Taylor points out that Clinton originated from the climes of the American South easily heard in his regional accent, for Bill Clinton was born in Arkansas.

Taylor makes a bold attempt to compare and contrast Clinton's ascendency to that of Kennedy. In 1960, Kennedy was forty-three when he was elected the thirty-fifth president of the United States. In 1992, Clinton was forty-six when he was elected the forty-second president of the United States. Taylor compares and contrasts the presidents' proximity in ages. What is more, Taylor makes his audience aware that these men were young leaders of their respective generations. Both were Ivy-League educated: Kennedy was a Harvard graduate; Clinton was a Georgetown graduate. They differed in many ways, including social and economic backgrounds, but we are focused on Clinton's graduation from Yale Law School.

We find significance in Taylor's use of the phrase "a lawyer meets a savior." It may have been heard as "Clinton the lawyer meets a savior" or "We who are lawyers meet a savior" or "I the lawyer meet a savior." We reinforce here that "the art of memory is better understood as a function of linking ideas through word pictures (mental mapping)." Taylor relies on his audience's keen literacy that he has identified them as characters in his narrative. In short and brilliantly, he has linked together concepts and ideas through word pictures, intersecting the Ivy-League educated with socioeconomic and political privilege. Taylor pointed toward the "privileged lawyers" as representatives of young, privileged Americans now in power and now responsible for providing leadership to the nation's hopes and dreams of a rebirth of its democratic ideals.

Taylor employs Clinton as a metaphoric trope. By this we mean a symbol, a representative of the new generation's lawyerly power and privilege. Indeed, the lawyerly crowds of Clinton's supporters are metaphoric symbols. They are living word pictures employed to link ideas at an intersection where the art of memory and narrative meet. The intersection provides rhetorical space for Taylor. He utilizes it to make his lawyerly crowds a part of his narrative as he invites them to ask silently what it all means. To be rhetorically successful, Taylor must persuade his audience to identify themselves as a part of Clinton's power and privilege, and second, Taylor must find a way not only to praise the newly elected president and the lawyerly crowds but also to advise them. For this, we turn to Kenneth Burke's identification and Roger D. Abraham's signification arguments:

> Identification is a key term in . . . analysis of rhetoric. Here the analytical tools of the grammar are brought to bear in understanding how the texts and performance are seen in relation to an audience. The reader, the listener, the observer is persuaded to something by the way of changing the identity of the object by its transformation to something else.[22]

> Signifying [signification] seems to be a Negro term, in use if not in origin. It can mean . . . the trickster's ability to talk with great innuendo, to carp, cajole, needle, and lie. It can mean in other instances the propensity to talk around a subject, never quite coming to the point. It can mean making fun of a person or situation. Also it can denote speaking with the hands and eyes, and in this respect encompasses a whole com-

plex of expressions and gestures. Thus it is signifying to stir up a fight between neighbors by telling stories; it is signifying to make fun of a policeman by parodying his motions behind his back; it is signifying to ask for a piece of cake by saying "my brother needs a piece of cake."[23]

We cannot definitively ascertain whether Taylor has consciously made use of Burke's identification and Abraham's signification to shape and develop his sermon's narrative. It is a segue, however, that draws immediate attention to the fact Clinton the lawyer becomes Clinton the lawyer in the narrative in the Gospel of Luke.

This is an example of how identification functions. Identification is a dynamic rhetorical tool that helps orators and preachers make audiences aware of the narrative's characters and that they share the narrative's characteristics and similarities. Of import here, we see that Taylor has created an intersection between the biblical narrative's lawyerly character and the lawyerly crowds present who now find themselves a part of the narrative that Taylor has created: "A lawyer, appropriately enough, asked the question, and I take it that that craft is not underrepresented here today, 'What shall I do to inherit eternal life?'"

Taylor gives voice to the lawyer. The lawyer becomes a living and breathing vicarious person who asked, "Why are we here? What is our purpose? We come out of darkness into this lighted room. What is the significance of it? What is the meaning of the high hope that lifts in our hearts and the dreams that people our days and the sense of purpose? What does it all mean?" This is consistent with the questions posed to Jesus of Nazareth in Luke's parable: "Teacher, what must I do to inherit eternal life?" and "Who is my neighbor?" Jesus understands that the lawyer's privilege may prohibit her or him from hearing that self-righteousness, however innocently derived, cannot justify unintended and irreparable damages imposed upon defenseless people. People seeking power for what they determine to be right causes is clearly, unmistakably sin when it results in collateral damages.

In response, Jesus tells the privileged lawyer a parable about a poor person left to die. Taylor claims as his own the rhetorical strategy and theological motif of the writer of Luke. For Taylor and for Jesus of Nazareth, it is an ethical imperative to use race, economic, political, and (white women's) gender privilege to help the oppressed and guarantee to them their democratic equality. There are differences in gender privilege, and most women of color are not privileged to have it.[24]

This lies at the taproot of Taylor's argument. He dresses his naked narrative with appealing and attractive clothing, which is his argument. The clothing makes his argument plausible and his narrative persuasive. In short, the lawyerly crowds will not discover the meaning of life until their privilege is used to reaffirm to the poorest their dignity and humanity among the privileges of the wealthiest—and for Taylor, this defines the intent and purpose of the nation's founders, which is to build an ever-increasingly inclusive democracy.

We suggest that it is plausible that Taylor has employed what Abraham has defined as signification. As Abraham argues, this is a tool that is available to the oppressed. Abraham's signification provides agency to the voiceless and powerless. "It can mean in other instances the propensity to talk around a subject, never quite coming to the point." We do not mean that Taylor preached around his audience; we suggest that Taylor understood how to be adroit—he wanted the lawyerly class to hear him. Otherwise; he would have titled his sermon "A Lawyer Meets a Savior."

Nonetheless, we offer this as this brief narrative summary. We assert that it provides a plausible context for Taylor stating that "a lawyer meets a savior." This in our view appears to be Taylor's intention. That is, he identifies Clinton with Kennedy; he signifies that Clinton the lawyer should seek Jesus of Nazareth as the lawyer does in Luke's parable. Taylor's volley of questions then may be directed toward his audience in general but directly toward Clinton and those like him in specific. Now that Clinton has become president, what does it mean? What can it mean? What should it mean? These are questions that point to what we call the Jesus ethic.

Of course identification and signification are symbols of experience. Taylor's comparison and contrast is general and meant to be broad and for the sole purpose to catch everyone present in a metaphoric net. However, we assert further that Taylor uses "symbol" to make an appeal to the newly elected young president to find the meaning of life by using his privilege to pursue the rebirth of democratic ideals. Taylor achieves this by his use of what we call signification:

> The symbol is perhaps most overwhelming in its effect when the artist's and the reader's patterns of experience closely coincide [Clinton the lawyer and other lawyers present] . . . The symbol [identification and signification] may also serve to force patterns upon the audience [we suggest this was Taylor's rhetorical strategy]; however, the universal experiences being capable of other grouping patterns than those which characterize the particular reader.[25]

It is a segue to Luke's parable about a lawyer who meets Jesus of Nazareth. We notice that Luke 10:25-28 shares a similarity in symbols of experience with the description of the rich young ruler who appears nearly in the same way as Luke's lawyer. The narrative about the rich young ruler is located in all of the Synoptic Gospels (Matthew 19:16-30; Mark 10:17-31; Luke 18:18-30). The ruler and the lawyer are presumably wealthy, privileged, and well-educated young men. In each instance, both asked Jesus of Nazareth existential questions about how to inherit eternal life. What is the meaning of life, and how do religious values intersect with secular ideals about the meaning of life?

This intersection has a long and storied history that can be traced well into Western civilization's past. We shall notice universal values of Western culture, namely, public spirit, true love of virtue, happiness, sensibility of the great blessings that flow from them, and the spirit of freedom. These themes are present in the United States Declaration of Independence: "we hold these truths to be self-evident, that all people are created equal. That they are endowed . . . by their Creator"; we notice these claims are made in the following excerpt that mirrors Western civilization's romanticism with Providence (America's adroit claims that this nation is founded by the providence of God). What follows is an example. It is similar to the content that became the United States Declaration of Independence:[26]

> THE RISING GLORY OF THIS WESTERN HEMISPHERE IS already announced; and she is summoned to her among the nations of the earth. We have publically declared ourselves convinced of the destructive tendency of standing armies. We have acknowledged the

necessity of public spirit and the true love of virtue, to the happiness of any people; and we profess to be sensible of the great blessings that flow from them. Let us not then act unworthily of the reputable character we now sustain. Let integrity of heart, the spirit of freedom, and rigid virtue be seen to actuate every member of the commonwealth.[27]

Because of a Deity's providence, the writer claims, "We have acknowledged the necessity of public spirit and the true love of virtue, to the happiness of any people; and we profess to be sensible of the great blessings that flow from them." The writer insists that appreciative and commonly held integrities demand a benevolent society. This seems to be at the heart of Eurocentric romanticism about its place in the world.

Of course, the majority classes and culture have been challenged over their historic interpretation and application of the nation's secular religious documents—and particularly the American Negro:

It is time that we stopped our blithe lip service to the guarantees of life, liberty and the pursuit of happiness. These fine sentiments are embodied in the Declaration of Independence, but that document was always a declaration of intent rather than of reality. There were slaves when it was written; and there slaves when it was adopted; and to this day, adopted; and to this day, black Americans have not life, liberty nor the privilege of pursing happiness, and millions of poor white Americans are in economic bondage that is scarcely less oppressive. Americans who genuinely treasure our national ideals, who know they are still elusive dreams for all too many, should welcome the stirring of the Negro demands. They are shattering the complacency that allowed a multitude of social evils to accumulate. Negro agitation is requiring America to reexamine its comforting myths and may yet catalyze the drastic reforms that will save us from social catastrophe.[28]

Martin Luther King Jr. was one of the twentieth century's most effective antagonists and critics of white hegemonic interpretation, narrative, and application of America's secular religious documents.[29] This helps readers to place into context the foreknowledge that Taylor possessed before he came to Clinton's inauguration worship service. Taylor would have known the historical differences that existed and exists between schools of interpretation of the Declaration of Independence and other secular religious documents.

Thus the foreknowledge that he possessed provides a window into how Taylor crafted his sermon, that is, how he intersected his art of memory and his narrative. We suggest that Taylor sought to make the Declaration something new—something that he hoped would rebirth the nation's intent to achieve all citizens' full inclusion in America's democracy. In order to do so, Taylor would need a rhetorical strategy that was similar to those who came before him.

We mentioned earlier that notable figures such as Frederick Douglass, Edward Everett, and Abraham Lincoln commonly used this style and species of rhetoric and narrative. We point toward Douglass's "What to the Slave Is the Fourth of July" and Lincoln's Gettysburg Address as clear examples.[30] We locate Taylor's sermon squarely in the center of this rhetorical tradition. Like those of the nineteenth century, Taylor in the twentieth century had been called upon to deliver a similar type of sermon discourse. In short, Taylor was familiar with the expectations that are associated with high-profile occasions. However, this occasion was special indeed. Taylor was called upon to deliver a civic sermon before the president-elect of the United States, William Jefferson Clinton, and ultimately the entire world.

What Taylor does differently than his predecessors is to bend time and impose upon the Declaration of Independence a new interpretation similar to what Lincoln achieves in the Gettysburg Address, which was a challenge for a national rebirth. New interpretation leads to new meaning. By this, we mean that Taylor created a different space in order to present the Declaration of Independence's new purpose and intent. Taylor then resets America's memory and identity with his version of what should have taken place.

> That national histories are not sets of established facts but rather socially constructed narratives of the past is widely accepted in academic circles today. Popular historical narratives are not unbiased descriptions of events but subjective accounts shaped by the present needs and interests of societies. While history may be "a fable agreed upon," the manner in which historical narratives are constructed has social and political significance. The process by which societies collectively develop and accept myths about the past that become their national history is not benign.[31]

We take seriously the claim that national narratives can create fables, and moreover, national narratives have social and political significance and can be lesser and larger subjective accounts.

In this way, we understand that Taylor had to reframe the founders' declaration. At the outset, America's founders failed to accomplish inclusion of all Americans into the nation's democracy. This failure led to four million slaves of African descent enduring more than 250 years of chattel slavery, another century of Jim Crow and Jane Crow, and to date, without retribution and restorative economic justice. Native Americans were systematically and brutally displaced from their native lands and faced near genocide. Women were denied their rights to vote and equal citizenship by law. In other instances, women by law could not own land. People who are not heterosexual have suffered indecencies that have not been socioeconomically and politically abolished.

Thus, Taylor, who understands Douglass's abolitionism and who participated in King's movement, now must reframe the nation's secular ideals and make them his own. This is a solid example of Taylor's use of the intersection between the art of memory and narrative. We reinforce here that narrative persuades. His way forward was to assume that these ideals have buoyancy. He does this in the following way: his narrated world is the world of the characters and it is narrated by the narrator. To be precise, his sermon content provided a different and new interpretation of the nation's founding characters.

What is precise also, Taylor preached about an America to come. This is eschatological or what is commonly understood as a vision of the future. In short, Taylor spoke of the nation's future as though already it is a fully contrite and a mature nation, a nation that forms its fully inclusive democracy based on his new interpretation of its declarations informed by the present needs and interests of societies. Taylor did so because he was the narrator of the narrative.

This is meant to underline Taylor's adroit use of the arts of invention and memory that intersect with his narrative. He created a narrative of realized (eschatological) hope for American democracy. As Taylor preached, his narrative, informed by his biblical text (Luke 10:25-28), creates a new American identity and destiny. The new American narrative is an inclusive democracy (it is now but it is not yet).

Taylor persuades his audience then to acknowledge and appropriate his realty with him.[32] In other words, Taylor became the embodiment of the narrative. Richard Lischer made similar comparisons when thinking about Martin Luther King Jr. King, according to Lischer, symbolically became the movement. "When an interviewer suggested to former aide C. T. Vivian that at the end of his life King was searching for his place in the Movement, Vivian responded incredulously, 'Man, Dr. King was the Movement.'"[33]

Whatever the case, there was no mistake. Taylor was someone whose words were to be heard and closely listened to.[34] After a preparatory prayer, Taylor came to the pulpit lectern. He made humorous and laudatory remarks, and with an unassuming ease, he began to deliver his sermonic discourse. From that time forward, he was in command of his audience.

Taylor's oratorical skills were on full display. His audience was thrilled in part by Taylor's brilliance and in part by his ability to recall long passages from memory. Taylor did not use written notes. His audience was witness to this, and in response it demonstrated noticeable appreciation for his oratory. President-elect Clinton was amazed while Taylor seemed to personify the intents of democracy's full-throated claims.

Taylor now comes to is penultimate example of how a word picture is at the intersection of the art of memory and narrative. It is his oral recitation of the first two paragraphs of the Declaration of Independence, America's most sacred secular religious document. We make note to readers the recital's location. The first two paragraphs of the Declaration are arranged and organized in a deliberate manner. Taylor's recitation from memory is meant to be showy. It is Taylor's artifice and ornamentation that bring pleasure to his hearers. However, it is more. It is a powerful word picture that invokes national consciousness and collective memory. By reciting the passages of the Declaration of Independence, Taylor has transformed his audience into one empathetic body of believers.

Taylor flashes his brilliance and performs what we can only describe as nothing less than the penultimate example of the art of memory's intersection with narrative—it is persuasive. Taylor's mental mapping and verbal action further endear him to his audience.

Taylor has become a living oracle, a person who can see the future and reframe it for his audience. This is the art of memory and how it intersects with narrative:

> You remember how the Declaration begins? "When, in the course of human events, it becomes necessary for one people to dissolve their political bands that have connected them with another, and to assume among the powers of the earth the separate and equal station which the laws of nature and of the nature's God entitled them, a decent respect of the opinions of humankind requires that they should declare the causes which impel them to the separation." And then these words, "we hold these truths to be self-evident, that all"—people, they really should have said—"are created equal." That they are endowed, not by any legislative act, not by any parliament, not by royal edict, but are "endowed by their Creator with certain unalienable rights."[35]

Gary Wills, the author of *Lincoln at Gettysburg*, wrote, "The Declaration of Independence has replaced the Gospel as an instrument of spiritual rebirth."[36] On this occasion, we assert that Taylor had a similar understanding that the nation was presented with another possibility of a rebirth. This, we contend, influenced his rhetorical strategy. In this instance, it is a Douglass-like and Lincolnesque definition of rebirth that Taylor has employed to make his claim that the nation's democratic promises must be renewed and offered to all citizens. In this way, we take note of Taylor's claims. That is, Taylor's sermonic claims are that the nation has been given an opportunity to experience yet another rebirth of liberation.

Furthermore, Taylor's recital provides him rhetorical space to challenge his audience to understand the significance of that historical period and context and how that period intersects with the current lawyerly generation's new period. It is a period where Providence has emerged and demands that the lawyerly crowds be engaged. This new historic period was theirs, and the providential period challenged the privileged and newly appointed to accept their new assignment.

His audience's assignment was to participate in the noble task of expanding and guaranteeing democratic rights for future generations of Americans. Their expansion and guarantee would be an example and beacon light of hope to the world. In order to do so, Taylor employed his recital of portions of the Declaration to remind his audience that its ancestors believed it was necessary to prosecute a war against its oppressor (England). Heretofore, like Douglass and Lincoln before him, Taylor would inspire his audience to engage in a war, but this time a war that continues as a war of ideas.

Each generation then must recognize hegemonic oppressive tactics and that these tactics are devised and sanctioned by their supporters. Supportive lawmakers pass laws and policies that lean toward certain privileged classes, genders, and even races of people. By reimagining the nation's original intent, contemporary and future citizens must remember that rebirth includes a new national consciousness and collective memory. These are necessary to grasp before citizens enter into the public debate. Their arguments must be reinforced with a persuasive message, which is that democracy must be fought for and protected. Citizens must be remembering that national consciousness and collective memory are integral aspects of the national narrative. Narrative persuades.

What follows is instructive. We have included four paragraphs from Taylor's civic sermon to provide context for our readers. The first paragraph states clearly Taylor's sermon thesis. He presents it as a treasure—a truth hidden in a field. Those who seek for it will discover this priceless treasure. Paragraph 2 is the recital of the Declaration, which functions as artifice, ornament, and word picture. Underneath these is Taylor's sermon goal. Taylor brings to the memory of his lawyerly crowd the new national identity and the new national consciousness, both of which point toward rebirth. The third paragraph is Taylor's advice to the lawyerly crowds and to president-elect Clinton: Do not repeat the vulgar and shameful atrocities that have occurred in other world places that demeaned Catholics and Jews and Southern Europeans.

In this same paragraph, Taylor makes a herculean theological leap. He suggests that the founders were aware of God's providence, and as time progressed, the nation's religious secular documents would be interpreted differently. By that we mean Americans would debate politics, religion, and culture and its need to change. The understanding of religious sacred documents would change as the culture changed. For Taylor, this was the assignment particularly for the privileged lawyerly class. Wage a war of ideas and change. People spearhead democratic changes for all those found in demeaning human conditions.

The fourth paragraph points toward Taylor's optimism that America would admit that its original sin was the tyranny of slavery. This is the penultimate example of democracy: democracy affords to its citizens the right to admit that it has endorsed previously wrongful doing. Taylor argues that to disagree with this premise may be nearly a treasonous act against Providence's and the founders' original intent for the reason of America. The American lawyerly class's assignment is to advance democratic rights to all citizens and ultimately the world.

Paragraph 1 is Taylor's sermon thesis:

> We are here to establish before the world that people can be brought together. And that highest and most difficult undertaking that can be known to the community of men and women can take place, that people can govern themselves. This is the American proposition in history. I need nobody to tell me what the original intent of this land was. It was that there should be an open democracy with liberty and justice for all. Argue as you will, but that is the purpose of America. I know because in our founding doctrines, those who set them down refused to admit anything less, however short were our actualities.[37]

Paragraph 2 is Taylor's recital of the first two paragraphs of the Declaration:

> You remember how the Declaration begins? "When, in the course of human events, it becomes necessary for one people to dissolve their political bands that have connected them with another, and to assume among the powers of the earth the separate and equal station which the laws of nature and of the nature's God entitled them, a decent respect of the opinions of humankind requires that they should declare the causes which impel them to the separation." And then these words, "we hold these truths to be self-evident, that all"—people, they really should have said—"are created equal." That they are endowed, not by any legislative act, not by any parliament, not by royal edict, but are "endowed by their Creator with certain unalienable rights."[38]

Paragraph 3 is Taylor's argument against political, religious, and racial biases:

How tempted they must have been to file exceptions. All except, all except Southern Europeans, all except Catholics, all except Jews. I will not use any more glaring examples. But they dared to placard before history "all people." They were not dissemblers, and they were not ignorant of the circumstance. They believed that time and God and intent of the nation would erase the stain in which they lived and about which a man said that the issue of race, of slavery, lay like a sleeping serpent coiled beneath the table of the constitutional convention. If you come down to our earthier document, our Preamble puts it—was it by accident?—"to establish justice" and then, "to ensure domestic tranquility." That was the order.[39]

Paragraph 4 is Taylor's argument that the founders believed in progressive revelation:

They refused to put the hated word slavery, the shameful word, in our Constitution. Over and over again, the reference is made to persons, even when the reference is made to three-fifths of a person, which I have never quite understood. I know who they were, but I don't know what they were. Three-fifths! They believed, under God, that history and time and justice would erase those stains. This leads me to the belief that this nation, though not divine, is divinely appointed. And I say to you solemnly today, that anybody who speaks or acts against that purpose or acts against the original intent that this shall be an open democracy with liberty and justice to all, comes close to continuing treason against the idea of America.[40]

Taylor's strategy then parallels Wills's proposition about rebirth. He reminds his audience that the nation was founded upon rebellion and resistance against hegemonic power: "it becomes necessary for one people to dissolve their political bands that have connected them with another." Second, Taylor knows the founders reasoned that their authority to disband from political hegemony was grounded in natural law, believing that "God entitled them" to separate from England because of dehumanizing treatment and unfair laws. Third, Taylor uses the Declaration to argue that equality is a God-given right: "We hold these truths to be self-evident, that all . . . are endowed by their

Creator with certain unalienable rights." This too can be construed as natural revelation. Finally, Taylor claims that the founders' original intent is to each generation. It must continue to engage in the ultimate goal, which is forging an American future that pursues an "open democracy with liberty and justice for all." Otherwise, Taylor claims, not doing so is "close to treason against the idea of America."

Taylor's art of memory and narrative are similar to that of Lincoln at Gettysburg. Both wanted the nation's citizens to embrace American rebirth and to embrace America's capacity to change—this is at the taproot of the founding documents. Unlike Lincoln, however, Taylor speaks through a lens of the oppressed. Taylor's rhetorical strategy then is similar to that which Jacqueline Bacon calls jeremiad rhetoric (we add that we see similarities in Thomas More's and Machiavelli's praise and advice, and Aristotle's praise and blame).[41] The jeremiad rhetoric points out that "the linguistic models of those in power claim to define marginalized members of society without acknowledging their perceptions, leaving them 'voiceless' in terms of the dominant group's discourse."[42]

Bacon is correct to focus on what it means to be voiceless. Simply, she describes what it means to be muted. "Mutedness does not connote silence, however; instead muted . . . must adopt linguistic strategies that allow them to speak for themselves in spite of their marginalized positon."[43] We cannot confirm that Taylor believed himself to be voiceless or muted, but we can confirm that he was aware that many people of African descent and other sociomarginalized people are voiceless and muted by the dominant culture's narrative. This was on full display as he preached a civic sermon to Washington's insiders and politicos, the lawyerly crowds who would meet a savior.

In short, for Taylor, his rhetorical strategy provides authoritative space for those who are not a part of the dominating race and culture's social norms. This political, economic, and socioracial construct protects hegemonic power. This kind of construct oppresses and mutes people, rendering them as invisible. What remains necessary is to reimagine and transform these constructs into pathways toward inclusivity for all citizens of the land. This is what justice looks like in real time and space.

Conclusion

We end where we began, by remembering our four admissions. First, we conceded that the conventional understanding of the art of memory, the rarest skill of memorization, is a skill that is possessed and mastered by only a few orators and preachers. We further restate that Gardner Taylor is among them. Second, we restate that the art of memory is the least written about and the least understood. We have argued that an expectation developed for ancient orators to demonstrate their abilities to recite long public addresses from memory. However, and third, we now know that memorization skills are a mental process between the brain and mind. All may not be endowed with this ability, but all can use other means to be effective communicators and preachers. And fourth, because of technological advancements, we have rethought our definition of the art of memory and how it functions in the context of the twenty-first century. We no longer need to memorize long public addresses, due in large part because of contemporary technical advances that provide assistance to orators and preachers who make public addresses (sermons). This task is easier because memorization skills are not necessary for contemporary audiences. Therefore we have redefined and reimaged that when the art of memory intersects with narrative, we are able to persuade audiences. We suggest strongly that preachers will be effective when we learn how to develop narratives with word pictures that help us link ideas and concepts.

We understand that when the art of memory and narrative intersect, words pictures are at the center of the intersection. Word pictures enhance our narrative content, and it is narrative that persuades. If people can remember our word pictures, people will remember our sermon narratives. Remember, narrative persuades. Finally, the art of memory can be learned not by developing memorization skills alone but by creating word pictures that serve as markers. Markers chart our sermon discourse both for the preachers and for our listeners. Gardner Taylor was gifted, even blessed, with a good memory. Our analysis of the art of memory, however, will improve our ability to bless our audiences' memory of our sermon content.

Epigraphs

Edward P. J. Corbett and Robert J. Connors, *Classical Rhetoric for the Modern Student*, 4th ed. (Oxford: Oxford University Press, 1999), 22.

Gardner C. Taylor, "Interview with Gardner C. Taylor," in *The Words of Gardner Taylor*, comp. Edward L. Taylor, vol. 5: *Lectures, Essays, and Interviews* (Valley Forge, PA: Judson Press, 2001), 280.

NOTES

1. Lane Cooper, *The Rhetoric of Aristotle* (Englewood, NJ: Prentice-Hall, 1932), xxiii.

2. Ibid., 9.

3. Ibid.

4. Kenneth Burke, *On Symbols and Society*, ed. Joseph R. Gusfield (Chicago: University of Chicago Press, 1989), 13.

5. Barbara Tversky, *Mind in Motion: How Action Shapes Thought* (New York: Basic Books, 2019), 34. Tversky theorizes that memory or mapping or "thinking is mental actions on mental objects—ideas. Actions on ideas that transform them into something else" (86).

> Much of . . . learning happens while the brain is maturing. People who were born blind and gain sight as adults can't make heads or tails out of what they see, a surprising and often wrenchingly disappointing outcome. Fortunately, blindness from birth has become far less frequent, and with training and experience, some visual competence can be acquired if sight is restored later in life. (34)

6. Ibid., 68.

7. Edward P.J.J. Corbett and Robert J. Connors, *Classical Rhetoric for the Modern Mind 4th Edition* (Oxford: Oxford University Press, 1999), 22

8. Gary Wills, *Lincoln at Gettysburg: The Words That Remade America* (New York: Simon & Schuster, 1992), 23.

9. Ibid., 24.

10. Ibid., 33–34.

11. Edward P. J. Corbett and Robert J. Connors, *Classical Rhetoric for the Modern Student*, 4th ed. (Oxford: Oxford University Press, 1999), 22.

12. Wills, *Lincoln at Gettysburg*, 42. See also Cooper, *Rhetoric of Aristotle*, xxxi, for a characterization of Lincoln's Greek rhetorical influences; see David W. Blight's introduction in *The Columbian Orator: Containing a Variety of Original and Selected Pieces Together with Rules, Which Are Calculated to Improve Youth and Others, in the Ornament and Useful Art*

of Eloquence, ed. David W. Blight (New York: New York University Press, 1998), xxv. Blight's excerpt speaks to the power that Douglass harnessed through his constant study of *The Columbian Orator*.

Wills writes:

Everett [was] considered by some the new Pericles for a young democracy of the Western world. Ralph Waldo Emerson, who studied Greek at Harvard in Everett's classroom, was emphatic in his teacher's praise: "There was an influence on the young from the genius of Everett which was almost comparable to that of Pericles in Athens."

Cooper writes,

This celebrated speech [the Gettysburg Address] is a good hunting-ground for illustrations of Aristotle's Rhetoric; so good, in fact, that a complete analysis of the speech by his principles would here be unwieldy. Reversing the order of the Rhetoric, let us briefly touch on salient points in Arrangement [mental mapping] (Taxis) and the Diction (Lexis) of the speech, and then on the argument (Dianoia) and the Ethos; not much need be added on Emotion. Aristotle begins with the internal form of a speech, and does not take up the external form until Book 3. In examining a particular specimen, we begin from the outside, with the visible quantitative parts.

Blight writes,

In spite of [Caleb] Bingham's argument that oratory—the mastery of language—is the challenge to "make the best use of what nature has bestowed upon us," speech is, as Garry Wills has stated, "unnatural" and "artificial." Words are inventions of the human imagination, their eloquent and persuasive manipulation a human artifice. The orator, with his sometimes transcendent words, is not born; he learns and practices his craft. He can only imitate nature; he is not nature itself, not Lincoln at the "Gettysburg Address," not Douglass in his "What to the Negro Is the Fourth of July," and not Martin Luther King in the "I Have a Dream" speech. However prophetic and inspired, the greatest of orations are likely to be the product of long education, revised drafts, borrowed and reinvented words. Hence, we can observe how Douglass, the great and widely admired orator, was the product both of his considerable gifts and of a peculiar kind of what Bingham might have called "schooling."

13. Joseph Evans, *Lifting the Veil Over Eurocentrism: The Du Boisian Hermeneutic of Double Consciousness* (Trenton, NJ: Africa World Press,

2014), 161–62. The following passage further explains how character, settings, and plotlines help to shape and move a narrative's action.

> All narratives include characters, settings, and plotlines. Characters serve many purposes in a narrative; for example, they facilitate reader analysis of the narratives' content and substance. Settings are sometimes referred to as major events, and they may be called kernels; they also point readers toward characters in the setting. In addition, kernels are major events that suggest critical points in the narrative that force movement in particular directions. They cannot be left out of the narrative without destroying its coherence and meaning. Narratives also have minor plot events, which often involve developing characters. They are also referred to as satellites: they are the development or working out of the choices made at the kernels. What is more, satellites do not have to appear in the immediate proximity of the kernels to which they are linked; they may appear anywhere in the narrative.

14. Ibid., 162.

15. bell hooks, *Killing Rage: Ending Racism* (New York: Henry Holt and Company, 1995), 15–16.

16. George A. Kennedy, *Classical Rhetoric and Its Christian and Secular Tradition from Ancient to Modern Times*, 2nd ed. (Chapel Hill: The University of North Carolina Press, 1999), 110–11.

17. Gardner C. Taylor, "Interview with Gardner C. Taylor," in *The Words of Gardner Taylor*, comp. Edward L. Taylor, vol. 5: *Lectures, Essays, and Interviews* (Valley Forge, PA: Judson Press, 2001), 278. Taylor comments further, "Although I don't use it in the pulpit or memorize it, I write a full manuscript of every sermon I preach. Some of the material is lost in the actual delivery, but material I hadn't planned comes to me while preaching. The one makes up for the other" (279).

18. Cornel West, *Democracy Matters: Winning the Fight against Imperialism* (New York: Penguin Books, 2005), 21–22. What follows is a lengthy passage that places the civic sermon in a sociohistorical and sociopolitical context.

> No democracy can flourish against the corruptions of plutocratic, imperial forces—or withstand the temptations of militarism in the face of terrorist hate—without a citizenry girded by these three moral pillars of Socratic questioning, prophetic witness, and tragicomic hope. The hawks and proselytizers of the Bush administration have professed themselves to be the guardians of American democracy, but

there is a deep democratic tradition in this country that speaks powerfully against their nihilistic, antidemocratic abuse of power and that can fortify genuine democrats today in the fight against imperialism. That democratic fervor is found in the beacon calls for imaginative self-creation in Ralph Waldo Emerson, in the dark warnings of imminent self-destruction in Herman Melville, in the impassioned odes to democratic possibility in Walt Whitman. It is found most urgently and poignantly in the prophetic and powerful voices of the long black freedom struggle—from the democratic eloquence of Frederick Douglass to the soaring civic sermons of Martin Luther King Jr., in the wrenching artistic honestly of James Baldwin and Toni Morrison, and in the expressive force and improvisatory genius of the blues/jazz tradition, all forged in the night side of America and defying the demeaning strictures of white supremacy. The greatest intellectual, moral, political, and spirited resources in America that may renew the soul and preserve the future of American democracy reside in this multiracial, rich democratic heritage.

19. Gardner C. Taylor, "Facing Facts with Faith," *The Words of Gardner Taylor*, comp. Edward L. Taylor, vol. 4: *Special Occasion and Expository Sermons* (Valley Forge, PA: Judson Press, 2001), 116.

20. Ibid.

21. Ibid.

22. Burke, *On Symbols and Society*, 18.

23. Roger D. Abrahams, quoted in Henry Louis Gates, Jr., *The Signifying Monkey: A Theory of African-American Literary Criticism*, 2nd ed. (Oxford: Oxford University Press, 2014), 59.

24. Jacqueline Bacon, *The Humblest May Stand Forth: Rhetoric, Empowerment, and Abolition* (Columbia: University of South Carolina Press, 2002), 196. See Lawrence W. Levine, *Black Culture and Black Consciousness: Afro-American Folk Thought from Slavery to Freedom* (Oxford: Oxford University Press, 1977), 31; Jacqueline Grant, *White Women's Christ and Black Women's Jesus: Feminist Christology and Womanist Response* (Atlanta: Scholars Press, 1989), 212. An example of inequity in gender privilege can be traced to biblical interpretation, as Grant has written: "For African American women in particular, the Bible must be read and interpreted in the light of Black women's own experience of oppression and God's revelation within that context."

25. Burke, *On Symbols and Society*, 110.

26. Bacon, *The Humblest May Stand Forth*, 84. Bacon makes a competent argument about how an American of African descent transformed the content of the Declaration of Independence into a jeremiad for justice and equality:

> Douglass's reference to potential slave insurrection in terms of both "the example of the fathers of '76" and Christian principles demonstrates the strong connection in American culture between sacred traditions and the "secular religion" associated with texts and symbolism of the founding of America. As the Bible was an authoritative text of American religious tradition, the Declaration of Independence was often elevated in nineteenth-century rhetoric of religious significance in mythologizing the founding of America, idealizing the creation of a completely new nation dedicated to liberty and equality. This text was resonant for antebellum Americans, who debated its meaning and significance, often focusing particularly on its relevance to slavery and the rights of free African Americans.

27. Jonathan Mason, "Extract from an Oration Delivered at Boston, March 5th, 1780," in *The Columbian Orator: Containing a Variety of Original and Selected Pieces Together with Rules, Which Are Calculated to Improve Youth and Others, in the Ornament and Useful Art of Eloquence*, ed. David W. Blight (New York: New York University Press, 1998), 262.

28. Martin Luther King Jr., "A Testament of Hope," in *A Testament of Hope: The Essential Writings and Speeches of Martin Luther King Jr.*, ed. James M. Washington (New York: HarperOne, 1986), 315.

29. Ibid., 217. We have included here an excerpt from "I Have a Dream" (August 28, 1963):

> So we've come here today to dramatize a shameful condition. In a sense we've come to our nation's capital to cash a check. When the architects of our republic wrote the magnificent words of the Constitution and the Declaration of Independence, they were signing a promissory note to which every American was to fall heir. This note was the promise that all men, black men as well as white men, would be guaranteed the "unalienable" rights of "Life, Liberty, and the pursuit of Happiness."

30. D. H. Dilbeck, *Frederick Douglass: America's Prophet* (Chapel Hill: University of North Carolina Press, 2018), 85–87. What follows is Dilbeck's characterization of the importance of Douglass's "What to the Slave Is the Fourth of July?" which was delivered in Corinthian Hall in Rochester, New York, on July 5, 1852.

No single speech more completely captured the prophetic voice Douglass had refined throughout the late 1840's and early 1850's than his "What to the Slave Is the Fourth of July?" More than 500 people gathered at Corinthian Hall in Rochester, New York, on 5 July 1852 to hear what they surely thought would be a typical, celebratory address venerating America's independence and founding. Instead, in the style of the ancient Hebrew prophet [a jeremiad], Douglass delivered a fiery sermon—condemning America for its wickedness and oppression, calling upon it to atone for its sins, and pleading with its people to pursue the path of true righteousness by living according to its highest political and religious ideals.

Douglass recited Psalm 137:1-6a (King James Version):

By the rivers of Babylon, there we sat down, yea, we wept when we remembered Zion. We hanged our harps upon the willows in the midst thereof. For there they that carried us away captive, required of us a song; and they that wasted us required of us mirth, saying, Sing us one of the songs of Zion. How shall we sing the Lord's song in a strange land? If I forget thee, O Jerusalem, let my right hand forget her cunning. If I do not remember thee, let my tongue cleave to the roof of my mouth.

Wills, *Lincoln at Gettysburg*, 263; Corbett and Connors, *Classical Rhetoric for the Modern Student*, 212, 432–33. Corbett and Connors write, "Lincoln's *Gettysburg Address* and Pericles's *Funeral Oration*, two of the classic examples of epideictic utterance about soldiers from 'our side' who died in battle, impress us as being as eloquent and genuine now as they were the day they were delivered from the podium" (212). What is certain, Lincoln places his speech's theme in the "beneath" of the speech or what we call the undertow and subtow. Lincoln's theme is birth, testing, and death before rebirth. Something, or in this instance, someone dies so that a larger harvest of life or lives may come forth. What follows is Cooper's analysis: birth, death, rebirth (*Rhetoric of Aristotle*, xxxii).

Proem (Birth):
Four score and seven years ago our fathers brought forth on this continent, a new nation, conceived in Liberty, and dedicated to the proposition that all men are created equal.
Statement:
Now we are engaged in a great civil war, testing whether that nation, or any nation so conceived and so dedicated, can long endure. We are met on a great battle-field of that war.

Argument:

We have come to dedicate a portion of that field, as a final resting place for those who here gave their lives that that nation might live. It is altogether fitting and proper that we should do this.

Body (Death):

But in a larger sense, we cannot dedicate—we cannot consecrate—we cannot hallow—this ground. The brave men, living and dead, who struggled here, have consecrated it, far above our poor power to add or detract. The world will little note, nor long remember what we say here, but it can never forget what they did here. It is for us the living, rather, to be dedicated here to the unfinished work which they who fought here have thus far so nobly advanced. It is rather for us to be here dedicated to the great task remaining before us—that from these honored dead we take increased devotion to that cause for which they gave the last full measure of devotion—that we here highly resolve that these dead shall not have died in vain

Epilogue (Rebirth)

—that this nation, under God, shall have a new birth of freedom—and that government of the people, by the people, for the people, shall not perish from the earth.

31. Timothy Longman, *Memory and Justice in Post-Genocide Rwanda* (Cambridge: Cambridge University Press, 2017), 35.

32. Paul Ricoeur, *Time and Narrative*, 3 vols. (Chicago: University of Chicago Press, 1985), 2:88. Also see Bacon, *The Humblest May Stand Forth*, 8–9; John Tinkler, "Praise and Advice: Rhetorical Approaches in More's Utopia and Machiavelli's The Prince," *The Sixteenth Century Journal* 19, no. 2 (Summer 1988): 187–207; and Cooper, *Rhetoric of Aristotle*, 17.

33. Richard Lischer, *The Preacher King: The Word That Moved America* (Oxford: Oxford University Press, 1995), 192.

34. Wills, *Lincoln at Gettysburg*, 58.

Lincoln's self-deprecating contrast of his (and Everett's) words with the soldier's deaths seems to neglect the second aspect of the Attic orators' contrast—the necessity, nonetheless, for words to insure undying fame. But that is implied in the notion that the world's remembering: reports will multiply beyond the few words said at any one time, in tribute to a deed that makes words necessary as they are inadequate.

35. User Clip: A Great American Preacher, https://www.c-span.org/video/?c4534389/great-american-preacher.

36. Wills, *Lincoln at Gettysburg*, 88.

37. Taylor, "Facing Facts with Faith," 116–17.

38. User Clip: A Great American Preacher.

39. Taylor, "Facing Facts with Faith," 117.

40. Ibid., 117–18.

41. Bacon, *The Humblest May Stand Forth*, 83–84. We include the following excerpt that points toward Douglass's "What to the Slave Is the Fourth of July?" We take notice of Douglass's style and his appropriation of the jeremiad to underscore a similar approach employed by Taylor:

> Douglass affirms Christian principles, but he challenges the traditional interpretation given them by white religious leaders who counsel submission and deny equality. Through the form of the jeremiad, he exploits the power of Christianity to liberate the oppressed and bring down the guilty. White religious leaders, Douglass demonstrates, cannot control the implications of Christ's teachings; rather, the African American prophet can assume an authority that undermines their traditional interpretations of Christianity and articulates a new vison of God's plan.

See also Cooper, *Rhetoric of Aristotle*, 46. To further appreciate Taylor's approach to the jeremiad, we include Aristotle's "praise and blame," which is a focal point of epideictic rhetoric:

> We have next to discuss virtue and vice, the noble and the base; for these are the objects of praise and blame. And our discussion will at the same time make plain the means by which a speaker may produce in his audience the impression that he is of such and such a character; this, as we noted . . . is our second method of persuasion. With regard to virtue, the same means will enable a man to make people accept either himself or another as trustworthy. Now praise may be serious, or it may be trivial; or does it always concern a human being or a god, for often enough it is applied to inanimate things, or to some insignificant animal. Whatever is praised, one must obtain the materials of argument in the same way. So we must include such things in our discussion, though for purposes of illustration only.

42. Bacon, *The Humblest May Stand Forth*, 8.

43. Ibid.

6

The Finishing Touch
The Art of Delivery

Taylor is not so much a storyteller as an incisive and exciting performer of the text and a commentary on the state of the human soul. Stylistically, he has mastered the inventory of African-American pulpit rhetoric—understatement, the ponderous ingratiation, parallelism, antithesis, the prophetic stutter, peroration, and the adroit manipulation of thematic set pieces—all delivered in the voice like a pipe organ and without hint of artificiality or self-conscious artistry. —Richard Lischer

In the arena of history, where God has chosen to work and where this encounter that Thursday night following the hymn singing occurred, God has arranged that our pretenses will be pulled away from us. It seems to me that a person preaching the gospel today must declare that what happened on that Thursday night and the crucifixion on Friday is a supreme clue as to what evil can do and how God can turn its monstrous deeds to something most splendid and salvific.—Gardner C. Taylor

We have chosen to present for review Gardner Taylor's sermon discourse "Preaching in the Urban Situation" (John 26:30) because we think it is among the finest in the Taylor canon and because it affirms Richard Lischer's commentary about Taylor's arts of eloquence, style, and delivery. We suggest Lischer is correct to indicate that Taylor's pulpit work epitomizes the expectations of ancient and contemporary teachers of classical rhetoric. Rhetoric then is an informant to pulpit discourse because it has an objective to find its end in judgment. Put another way, rhetoric's objective is to persuade for a decision by an audience. In fact, classical rhetoric has three kinds of oratory: deliberative, forensic, and epideictic.[1]

Elements of Delivery

In this chapter, however, we will focus narrowly on the epideictic and even more narrowly on how it functions as praise and blame and praise and advice. Our first example points toward praise and blame and the second and third point toward praise and advice. We will notice that these overlap and are interrelated:

> The ordinary proem [introduction] for Epideictic . . . is a bit of praise or blame . . . "You deserve admiration far and wide, Men of Greece"— where he praises those who instituted the great festivals . . . Isocrates, on the other hand, censures them for bestowing honors on athletic prowess, but giving no prize at all to men who succeed in the things of the mind.[2]

> There is a specific interrelation between praise and advice; for anything you might suggest in a speech of advice can, by a shift in the expression, be turned into encomium. And so, when we know what should be done, and what a man ought to be, we must give to our utterance of these things as advice a shift around, and invert expression.[3]

> So the rule is this: When you wish to praise, consider what you suggest is advisable; and when you wish to advise, consider what would praise a man for doing.[4]

There is a brilliant New Testament example of praise and blame and praise and advice that is located in the rhetoric of Paul of Tarsus (1 Corinthians 15:50-58):

> What I am saying, brothers and sisters, is this: Flesh and blood cannot inherit the kingdom of God, nor can corruption inherit incorruption. Listen, I am telling you a mystery: We will not all fall sleep, but we will all be changed, in a moment, in the twinkling of an eye, at the last trumpet. For the trumpet will sound, and the dead will be raised incor-

ruptible, and we will be changed. For this corruptible body must be clothed with incorruptibility, and this mortal body must be clothed with immortality. When this corruptible body is clothed with immortality, and this mortal body is clothed with immortality, then the saying that is written will take place:

> Death has been swallowed up in victory.
> Where, death, is your victory?
> Where, death, is your sting?

The sting of death is sin, and the power of sin is the law. But thanks be to God, who gives us the victory through our Lord Jesus Christ! Therefore, my dear brothers and sisters, be steadfast, immovable, always excelling in the Lord's work, because you know that your labor in the Lord is not in vain.

We observe that praise and blame and praise and advice are located throughout this beautifully stitched, symmetrically quilted passage. At times these overlap. The apostle is eloquent and stylish; he praises the mysterious transformation (which he attributes to God) that takes place when the human body is deceased from biological and chemical life. "The dead will be raised incorruptible . . . the body must be clothed in incorruptibility . . . this mortal must be clothed in immortality" are examples from Paul's writing of praise and blame and praise and advice.

Paul of Tarsus claims that virtue belongs to the life giver, namely, God, but vice or blame belongs to sin. Here sin is described as a noun (a thing). The advice which the apostle gives is to the brothers and sisters to be "steadfast, immovable, always excelling in the Lord's work . . . you know that your labor in the Lord is not in vain." We can summarize praise and blame and praise and advice as virtue and vice. Of virtue, it is an orator or a preacher, in this instance, speaking well of someone, of an occasion, or even about an immobile object, a thing. By contrast, vice is used to accuse someone, to critique harshly an occasion, or quite possibly to accuse a thing. Of advice, it is an ethical judgment. It serves to suggest to an audience that there is a way forward.

Throughout the ages, rhetoricians have taught praise and blame and praise and advice to orators of all disciplines. Homileticians have taught Christian preachers of all traditions and sects to pursue, if not perfect, this art form. What many have taught and others have pursued we are firm in our judgment that praise and blame and praise and advice are forms of rhetoric that function throughout Taylor's pulpit discourse, "Preaching in the Urban Situation." We affirm what Lischer ascribes to Taylor: he possessed the rarest oratorical gift which informed his noble calling to persuade people to Christian faith. More, Taylor's Christian proclamation is underlined by ethical constructs. In this way, Taylor understood that it is ethical to stand on the side of the oppressed and resist unethical forms of oppression sanctioned by the guardians of institutional spheres and the public square.

"Preaching in the Urban Situation" is a clear example of how to deliver a sermon discourse in privileged spaces amid privileged professors and students, predominately white, during the last days and hours of the 1960s. Preachers will appreciate this sermon discourse because there are many exemplary aspects that warrant its lengthy and careful study. However, in this final chapter, we are focused on Gardner Taylor's arts of eloquence, style, and delivery. We begin, however, with a brief overview of the art of delivery.

The art of delivery is a broad subject. We suppose that like the other parts of rhetoric which are discussed in preceding chapters, the art of delivery is a subject that can fill volumes of books. Delivery or pronunciation is the fifth part of rhetoric. "Delivery, delivery, delivery," was considered the most important part of rhetoric by the great Greek orator Demosthenes.[5] Of course, we contend that our theory for the art of delivery is helpful. In addition, however, we bring to preachers' attention that they must engage in disciplined study of the great ancient and contemporary preachers and orators and devote constant care to the various parts of their sermons and speeches.

Certain parts are an *exordium*, which is an introduction; *narrative* is our preferred way to shape and inform an audience about the direction that a preacher wants to guide their discourse. We point out *digression*, which is similar to what Lischer describes as Taylor's ponderous ingratiation, parallelism, and prophetic stutter. In earlier chapters, we have made suggestions which provide ways for preachers to use a *proposition* and an *argument*. Last but not least and perhaps the most important part of a sermon is the *peroration*, which we refer to as an effective conclusion.

What is more, Taylor's art of delivery is an appropriate guide for those who are assigned to stand, argue, and persuade those who continue to benefit from biases sustained in the institutional spheres (e.g., the academy, policy think tanks, and related spheres of influence) and the public square (e.g., mass gatherings of activists). We keep in mind that institutions have influence upon institutions, and grassroots organizations and public mass movements have influence upon the public square. Thus, in this context, institutional spheres and the public square are metaphors. Metaphor here is a symbol of places where ethical possibilities are debated.

It is ethical to debate ideas; it is ethical to question authoritarian regimes; it is ethical to argue for human rights. It is ethical to debate institutional policy positions in the halls of Congress, the halls of higher education, the halls of the psychological associations and before leaders of our judicial branches. It is ethical to debate unfair labor practices and inadequate access to health care in rural counties, in rural states, in the local and national opinion editorial pages in the land. It is ethical to organize liberation marches and protest publically against or for an ethical position in the public square. It is ethical for preachers to debate these issues in these spheres and square. It is ethical for preachers to accept invitations to speak at business prayer breakfast meetings and accept invitations to speak at women's rights protest meetings. Wherever an ethical positon should be debated, preachers are to be in the middle of those ethical debates.

It is "the ethical" that lies at the taproot of the Judeo-Christian democratic tradition and non-Christian democratic traditions. The images that we hope come to mind are the ancient prophets and orators of the Hebrew, Christian, and Greco-Roman traditions. Among them are Demosthenes, Cicero, Paul of Tarsus, Sojourner Truth, Frederick Douglass, Martin Luther King Jr., Kwame Nkrumah, Winnie Mandela Jr., and Gardner Taylor. In a real sense, sacred and secular worldviews find nexus in a quest for human equalities and rights. Similar to the sermons that took place in the civil rights movement and era, throughout his pulpit work Taylor continued to preach in that democratic tradition.

Taylor's discourse which is under our review was delivered at Princeton Theological Seminary on November 20, 1969. We consider the academy an institutional sphere; we consider those who earn degrees in seminary education are persons who should embrace their bifocal lens. On the one hand, the educated are those empowered to speak in the spheres. On the other hand, the educated are those who are empowered to engage in the public square. Indeed, preachers should be able to address the masses, as you will soon see, in their own "tongues." Taylor was a part of these spaces, and he was capable of bridging the gap between the secular and sacred, the academy and the church, the spheres and the square.

On this occasion, Taylor's Princeton sermon discourse occurred approximately one year and a half after Martin Luther King Jr.'s assassination. This historical context adds to our understanding of Taylor's rhetorical situation. After a hymn was sung by male voices, in the glee club tradition, there was immediate silence. Only when Taylor began to walk across a hard-floor surface toward the pulpit lectern was the silence interrupted. Above the silence, we then hear Taylor's baritone voice rise. His audience was Princeton's academic faculty and seminary students. Throughout his sermon delivery, Taylor demonstrated that he was aware of his special audience.

Readers will notice that Taylor made tasteful use of the 1960s historical context and appropriated the 1960s culture as "signs of the times." The cultural upheavals became for Taylor a word picture which he used to frame and shape his sermon content. Taylor was savvy to include the raging external existential crisis that surrounded the privileged faculty and seminarians inside the protective citadel that was Princeton. He knew his audience, and he had predetermined how he would meet their expectations. In order to demonstrate this, we have included excerpts from that sermon discourse to provide a brief analysis of Taylor's lucid use of the arts of eloquence, style, and delivery.

The first excerpt is an example of Taylor's creative ability (his art of invention). We shall see his sermon's original idea and thesis, proposition, and argument crafted nearly as a unified expression. Taylor takes the existential crisis from the abstract and makes it plain to see. He clothes the crisis in a word picture: the violence of the 1960s.

In the second excerpt, Taylor segues from his sermon introduction toward his discourse's narrative. He skillfully reconstructs the scenes that took place in the upper room where Jesus keeps the Passover and institutes what is commonly called the Last Supper (Communion). He performs this shift seemingly without effort and adroitly.

> We are now within forty-two or forty-three days of the end of the decade of the 1960s. We are close on to the last thirty years of the century. And most of you will be spending your ministry in that thirty years, and please God, in the early portion of the twenty-first century. What is the angle and vision and thrust of the gospel that is particularly and peculiarly relevant for that generation to which you will be addressing the gospel of Jesus Christ? What are the tongues of this generation in which they might hear the gospel of their own language? A generation suckled upon violence and collapse and what has been widely called a post-Christian era, but what is perhaps more hopefully and more realistically a pre-Christian era.[6]

> In this passage of Scripture which you have heard this morning, there is a declaration of those twin aspects of the gospel peculiar to your generation and in a more general sense to my generation, but particularly to this. "And when they had sung a hymn they went out into the Mount of Olives" (Matthew 26:30). Now that first surely belongs to all generations. It is among the tenderest settings of the entire Bible and, indeed, of the whole sweep of a flickering candlelight, their faces caught in alternating lights and shadows as the flicker of the flames moves upward and downward with succeeding gusts of winds. One man, obviously their leader, is talking to them about some deep and ominous foreboding before him, all tied with a death almost too horrible to describe. It is of course Jesus talking to his disciples. The Christian community through the centuries has found in that event one of the most deeply moving experiences and recurrences of Christian life. He talks with them about this oncoming encounter.[7]

We find it significant how Taylor has crafted rhetorical boundaries that provide shape and add structure to his narrative. For example, he creates a historical timeline which points toward the end of the 1960s. He describes the 1960s as a violent decade. In fact, he has only to mention the word *violence* and it becomes its own word picture. The picture makes graphic how oppressors preyed upon the oppressed and sought to punish those who resisted imperial power.

More than that, Taylor points his audience through it. That is, he guides them through the violence of the decade. He accomplishes this by using his word picture as a guidepost. The timeline suggests that the future does exist invisibly, and surely it will become visible somewhere in the seminary students' collective future. Another part of Taylor's segue is toward the biblical text that is central to his narrative. Taylor achieves this by pivoting from his timeline to his biblical text by asking his audiences two penetrating rhetorical questions.

Taylor's first question, "What is the angle and vision and thrust of the gospel that is peculiarly relevant for that generation to which you will be addressing the gospel of Jesus Christ?" A second question follows: "What are the tongues of this generation in which they might hear the gospel in their own language?" In his third move, he makes a descriptive pronouncement that includes what may be his personal critique of the state of Christianity in the latter part of the twentieth century: "A generation suckled upon violence and collapse and what has been widely called a post-Christian era, but what is perhaps more hopefully and more realistically a pre-Christian era." Taylor's two questions and a personal critique are meant to probe well into his audience's hearts and minds in order to transform his audience of individuals into a single body. We are meant here to appreciate Taylor's narrative as a tasteful work of art, and as a thing of beauty. By this we mean Taylor has created an aesthetic narrative form that underlines its function.

There is another way to appreciate what Taylor has accomplished. We speculate, first, that Taylor's questions point to a Pentecost experience, "peculiar" and "tongues." Second, Taylor seems to lampoon American Christianity by subtle suggestions that an authentic American Christianity may have been birthed by the death of King. There is a new birth, a symbolic Pentecostal birth that has emerged. Taylor identifies the Pentecost birth by its peculiarities and multicultural tongues.

Despite our speculation, we concede that Taylor was deliberately unclear about what the peculiarities and tongues definitively mean. Are these symbols, ideas that are linked to post-Christian culture and pre-Christian culture? Does this mean that post-Christian culture is the death of Eurocentrism? By pre-Christian culture, does Taylor point to the Acts of the Apostles (Acts 2)? Do peculiarities parallel signs and wonders, and tongues parallel diversity of people in a multicultural and multiracial nation? Whatever the case, Taylor signifies that something has died and something else has been birthed. Taylor is a master of the arts of eloquence and style which inform and intersect his art of delivery.

Language, Tone, and Preparation

Let us remember that there is no straight line to follow. Taylor's use of the arts of eloquence, style, and delivery can be located in different ways throughout this sermon discourse. In this particular sermon introduction, we locate this intersection by taking notice of Taylor's carefully chosen words: "What is the angle and vison and thrust of the gospel that is particularly and peculiarly relevant for that generation?" Taylor links this first flash of peculiarity with "there is a declaration of those twin aspects of the gospel peculiar to your generation . . . (Matthew 26:30) . . . Now that the first surely belongs to all generations." Taylor has bridged the gap by repeating the word *generation*. This conjures a collective word picture. Of course this cannot be accomplished by beginning a sermon discourse with the highest volume, capacity, and energy of the human voice. In his Yale University Lyman Beecher Lecture (1922), Charles Reynolds Brown comments on the proper voice tone that preachers are to use in the early stages of their sermon discourse:

> The delivery of a sermon had best begin in an easy conversational tone. If you start immediately after the style of Spartacus . . . it will make it difficult for you to increase steadily the power and effectiveness of your delivery in the further development of your theme. Begin on the level even though you are proposing to carry the whole congregation up into the seventh heaven of spiritual ecstasy when the right moment comes. When I begin my sermon, especially in some strange church where I may never have preached before, I usually fix my eye on someone in the rear of the church, and may make my first remark

to him. If I can gain and hold his attention from the very start I may be fairly sure that I am winning a sympathetic hearing from all the rest. If the opening sentences of the sermon are not uttered too rapidly or in too loud a tone of voice this gives time for your vocal organs to adjust themselves to the task of delivery. The tone of dignified conversation furnishes the staple method for delivery. It wears better than any other style of speech. The men who shout and roar in the pulpit are not the men who speak to the human heart the words of eternal life.[8]

Unlike Brown, Taylor avoided explaining clearly how he constructs his sermon delivery. As you will read, Taylor admits that he did not formulate a homiletic sermon delivery method. We suggest, however, that Taylor came close to an agreement with Brown's approach:

> I can't give any formula for how I deliver a sermon; it depends on the sermon, on the mood of the preacher, on the mood of the congregation. Black preachers used to have a formula for it: "start low, go slow, get high, strike fire, retire". . . Once I get into the sermon, I try to get very close to the congregation. Any movement on their part, for example, bothers me greatly, because I have to feel they are right there with me. What I am delivering is not an abstract lecture but a communication about a life-and-death matter.[9]

We agree with Brown's and Taylor's pursuit of the right speakerly tone. A sermon delivery, we suggest, is persuasive when it is clothed by eloquence and style. Hugh Blair characterized this balance as a significant aspect of delivery. He claimed that an audience can be drawn to attention "when any great danger roused them, and put their judgment on trial, they commonly distinguished, very justly, between genuine and spurious eloquence." Citing the oratory of Demosthenes, Blair commented that Demosthenes "triumphed over all his opponents because he spoke always with a purpose, affected no insignificant parade of words, used weighty arguments, and showed them clearly where their interest lay."[10] Of course, Demosthenes spoke in the institutional spheres and the public square to persuade the course of history.

We expect similar convictions and pursuits from every preacher. Preachers address life-and-death issues weekly. What is more, preachers are challenged here to learn how to address "the ethical" and connect the dots between local and national issues and global affairs. This helps our audiences to understand how they fit into the interconnectedness of the world around them. This occurs in large part when preachers seriously take into their consideration the concerns of the people they serve. We must remember that people have daily anxieties and convictions. A preacher's mastery creates this kind of intersection, that is, where people's lives are interconnected with other people in the global community.

There are complex issues that preachers must address that require sociopolitical, socioreligious, and sociopsychological deftness. It is a preacher's deftness that makes her or him an effective communicator in institutional spheres and the public square. What is certain, a preacher who engages in the spheres and the square must be literate in many different disciplines and particularly in the science of politics. Adept preachers must ask, "Is this politic ethical? Is this politic democratic?" During the twentieth century, those who witnessed the civil rights struggles understood the role of religious activism and the sophisticated oratory of Martin King that influenced attitudes and behaviors in institutional spheres and the pubic square.

Gardner Taylor, because he was a participant in the civil rights movement, understood political complexities. His preaching reflects his understanding and commitment to remain a proactive religious activist. However, activism must be reinforced by sophisticated oratory.[11] Taylor had the rhetorical ability and mental capacity to engage in the ethical and democratic debates that raged in his time. These kinds of circumstances, we suggest, are what informed Taylor and led to how he shaped his sermon content and to an extent his sermon delivery. As a response, Taylor employed eloquence and style to clothe his narrative which he deployed in his sermon delivery to persuade guardians of the spheres and the square.

It seems clear that these factors are underneath this intersection that exists between Taylor's arts of eloquence, style, and delivery. For Taylor, these are an inseparable single chain stich. This stich is interwoven into the fabric of the narrative that underlies his delivery. We see these similarities in Blair's comments about eloquence and style. For Blair, eloquence and style are a writer's peculiar manner. We add that these same guidelines are appropriate to describe Taylor's peculiar manner:

When I entered on the consideration of style, I observed that words being the copies of our ideas, there must always be a very intimate connection between the manner in which every writer employs words, and his manner of thinking; and that from the peculiarity of thought and expression which belongs to him, there is certain character imprinted on his style . . . They arise from the whole manner of his language; and comprehend the effect produced . . . the choice which he makes of single words; his arrangements of these sentences; the degree of his precision; and his embellishment, by means of musical cadence, figures, or other arts of speech.[12]

Blair's definition of peculiar manner we associate with that of Taylor. We highlight here common words and phrases that are included in Blair's definition of peculiar manner with Taylor's common use of eloquence and style as seamless threads in his sermon delivery (language, single words, arrangements of sentences, precision and embellishment, and musical cadence).

Of equal importance, sermon delivery must be practiced in order for it to be improved. Improvement comes with familiarity, that is, with the discourse's content and structure and with how a preacher understands her or his discourse's rhythm, as Taylor indicates:

I practice [my sermon delivery] Saturday evening. I listen to spirituals and gospel music on my stereo. They help me get into a cadence . . . On Sunday morning, even before getting up, I like to go through my sermon in my mind to see what grasp I have of it . . . I read over my sermon three times; twice on Saturday, once to proof it because it has to be typed later, and the second time for absorption, and then once on Sunday before I leave the house . . . Language . . . The preacher has no excuse for unnecessarily sloppy language. Words must make definite suggestions, not only in their definitions but in their sound. There are words that caress, words that lash and cut, words that lift, and words that have a glow in them . . . Words are the currency in which the preacher deals; we must be very careful not to deal with them loosely, because if they are debated or devalued, there's no other currency we have in which to deal. A preacher should not worship at the altar of words, but he or she must have due regard and reverence for language.[13]

We now firmly attach Taylor's peculiar manner to his sermon delivery. By this we mean Taylor's sermon delivery is informed, as we previously mentioned, by eloquence and style. Expressed another way, Taylor's style is the art of eloquence. Eloquence and style shape and clothe Taylor's sermon delivery. We encourage all preachers to learn this practical approach. An excellent sermon delivery, however, does not begin without a deliberate decision to make this a part of a preacher's habit, study, and discipline. Clothing a sermon in eloquence and style without content does a grave disservice to all sermon discourses.

Transcending Boundaries

Cleophus LaRue is a consequential homiletician and author. LaRue, in *Rethinking Celebration,* has provided an incisive critique about the state of contemporary preaching in many of our churches. His study supports and points toward our position on some species of popularized and contemporary preaching. Sadly, we characterize some preachers' eloquence, style, sermon content, and delivery as unrefined, unpolished, and lacking in sermon preparation. Unpreparedness can be defined in many ways, but here it means ineffective and unpersuasive communication between the pulpit and the pew: "[A] clarion call for . . . preachers [is] to think more deeply about the aims and ends of their preaching—namely, to stop putting so much emphasis on celebratory endings to our sermons and focus more on the substantive content in our sermons."[14]

LaRue is not arguing in favor of an intentionally flat, pedestrian, uninteresting sermon discourse. To the contrary, LaRue argues for a corrective to our sermon delivery by challenging preachers to be more thoughtful about our sermon discourse's objectives and how it influences and affects audiences. Informed by LaRue, we acknowledge that there are certain kinds of sermon discourse that are parochial and organic, and perhaps appreciated only in specific cultural settings. As a consequence, these kinds of sermon discourse do not have currency and persuasive influence in institutional spheres and the public square.

These kinds of sermon discourses are effective in limited settings (as some sermons should be) but are not portable and transcending. It is our view that a discourse that transcends parochial boundaries is needed. What is more, we live in an increasingly biblically illiterate, complex, multicultural society. Pulpiteers who are not trained and equipped to communicate across parochial boundaries will not connect with highly technically advanced audiences, as LaRue argues:

> In the face of this nationwide numerical decline in organized religion and amidst a growing biblical illiteracy, our emotional rejoicing in worship grows stronger and stronger while our understanding of Scripture and theology seems to grow weaker and weaker. We are emphasizing emotional rejoicing too much and substantive content in sermons too little. Not only have we diluted the gospel through our lack of solid preparation for preaching, but all too many . . . preachers have privatized the faith, removed it from the public square, bought into some version of the prosperity gospel, and turned preaching into little more than motivated speech for the privatized longings of a consumer-oriented clientele.[15]

Few can dispute what LaRue describes as vaguely Christian proclamation. Of course, this is problematic, and if we accept LaRue's argument, this kind of sermon discourse will not reach current generations because many are conditioned by a complex, multicultural, and increasingly secular society. There is a glimmer of light, however. Preachers can be effective when we take seriously how Taylor's sermon delivery is informed by an intersection between the arts of eloquence, style, and delivery. What is more, preachers' efforts to learn and master this intersection will make us competitive for this generation's hearts and minds. Where do we compete? We compete in institutional spheres and the public square.

Before Frederick Douglass, Sojourner Truth, Abraham Lincoln, Martin Luther King Jr., and Gardner Taylor spoke in Christian tones in the spheres and square, Jesus of Nazareth did. No preacher created an intersection between the arts of eloquence, style, and delivery more effectively than the Nazarene. The penultimate example of such public square oratory is his Sermon on the Mount:

> Blessed are the poor in spirit,
> for the kingdom of heaven is theirs.
> Blessed are those who mourn,

for they will be comforted.
Blessed are the humble,
for they will inherit the earth.
Blessed are those who hunger and thirst for righteousness,
for they will be filled.
Blessed are the merciful,
for they will be shown mercy.
Blessed are the pure in heart,
for they will see God.
Blessed are the peacemakers,
for they will be called sons [and daughters] of God.
Blessed are those who are persecuted because of righteousness,
for the kingdom of heaven is theirs . . .

When Jesus had finished saying these things, the crowds were astonished at his teaching. (Matthew 5:1-10; 7:28a)

We take notice of how Jesus of Nazareth's arts of eloquence, style, and delivery take hold of us. One reason is the beauty and symmetry that shape and give structure to his sermon discourse. Another reason that we appreciate the Sermon on the Mount is that we see Jesus of Nazareth demonstrate our claim that an intersection of the arts of eloquence and style enhances sermon delivery. The writer claims Jesus of Nazareth has carefully and deliberately chosen his precise words that transcend time, space, and history. Jesus of Nazareth's words address a deeply felt emptiness in the hearts and minds of both his original ancient and contemporary audiences.

Jesus of Nazareth's words point toward a specific class of people who seem to be the focal point of his message. His sermon discourse was not delivered in a church adorned with historic stained glass windows. He preached in the public square, and there his sermon discourse touched the oppressed of every generation. These people were not of noble stock. These people were the disinherited people who will never find satisfaction in worldly wares: "poor . . . heaven is theirs . . . those who mourn . . . they shall be comforted . . . the humble . . . will inherit the earth . . . those who hunger and thirst . . . they shall be filled . . . the merciful . . . they will be shown mercy . . . the pure . . .

will see God . . . the peacemakers . . . will be called sons [and daughters] of God . . . those . . . persecuted . . . [heaven] is theirs." These words are language arranged to give people hope and point all toward the future—an explanation and declaration of the kingdom of God.

We do not claim that anyone in history will preach and communicate as effectively as Jesus of Nazareth. But in earthier tones all can learn the arts of eloquence and style and how these intersect with sermon delivery. This is not beyond our grasp with study, practice, and discipline. Nevertheless, we must remember that the objective of preaching is that truth take hold of us, "truth in the most advantageous light for conviction and persuasion."[16] Eloquence and style unlock human imagination. "Every sermon therefore should be a persuasive oration."[17] Thus, there is a species of discourse that is meant to be understood as consequential and rises above perceived immediacy and aims at transcending time and space. The intersection of the arts of eloquence and style with the art of delivery makes this possible.

Eloquence and style are not arts that should be used to confuse an audience. Instead, their utility is to make abstract concepts attractive but plainly understood. We are to remember here that a sermon's content is to persuade people that truth has come to light and the preacher is trusted as a conduit, a messenger of truth. If this is plausible, then an appropriate and proper art of delivery is essential. By that we mean that truth is attached to the preacher delivering the sermon's charge, whether that is instruction, illumination, insight, or inspiration. All of this points to the preacher and her or his sermon delivery. Much of this is accomplished by the preacher's disposition: an interesting manner undergirded with charming anecdotes and goodwill toward the audience. These qualities lead to perfecting an intersection between the arts of eloquence, style, and delivery.

The role of a preaching pastor is to preach eloquently with the hope that the oppressed will continue to resist empire. We who are oppressed may not feel that our oppression will cease in our lifetime. Still, we do need to know that our yearning is sanctioned and justified by our faith in Jesus of Nazareth. Eloquent preaching then arrests our yearning hunger and thirst for righteousness. Eloquent preaching is penetrating and liberating. Over time, eloquent preaching births a radical self-realization. Eloquent preaching that is delivered well is balanced by the prophetic foretelling about the present age.

An honest critique of our worldly conditions affirms our sense and sensibilities. As preachers, we must confirm to people that we are not insane or paranoid. Like Jesus of Nazareth in the Sermon on the Mount, we have a fiduciary duty to make clear that those who listen to us have the same fiduciary duty to grapple with and resist oppressive regimes in the world that we have inherited and will bequeath. Eloquent preaching is hopeful, and the sermon is a proposition and an argument to be made persuasively. We must remember that persuasive speech and preaching must be delivered in a present-future tense. Hope then is an investment into the future.

Through the ages, this concept of hope has been grasped by unnumbered faithful wayfarers: "After this I looked, and there was a vast multitude from every nation, tribe, people and language, which no one could number standing before the throne and before the Lamb. They were clothed in white [pure] robes with palm branches in their hands" (Revelation 7:9). This is an example of what the future looks like for those who continue to hope. Thus it is beneficial to preachers to learn how to create an intersection between the arts of eloquence, style, and sermon delivery.

This stands in stark contrast to that which disturbs LaRue. There are specific kinds of preaching that have gone awry. There are growing numbers of sermons that commonly miss the mark. However, there is a shaft of light that glimmers through the veil of ashen nihilism. There are sermons that hit the target's mark and provide a solid context that highlights the biblical passage's narrative and provide important exposition, underscored by demonstrating its timeless sociohuman relevance. All should be concerned over pulpit oratory that lacks ethical maturity and intellectual curiosity. Preachers are called and assigned to critique a culture that is void of empathy, empty of sociopolitical insight, and bankrupt of moral and ethical moral currency: "I . . . argue that effective preaching, by which I mean preaching that speaks powerfully to this present age while at the same time remaining true to sound scriptural/theological traditions, is being overshadowed by a misunderstanding of the place and significance of celebration."[18]

LaRue is concerned rightly about the shallowness we associate with much of today's sermon discourse content and delivery. By this, we mean we are plagued by continuous shallow discourses that lack biblical substance, theological depth, ethical direction, clarity, persuasive rhetoric and homiletic quality. If rudimentary rules of rhetoric are learned and followed, we suggest that our contemporary preaching will improve and once again, we will have thoughtful preachers who will avoid the temptation of amusing ourselves and our congregations to death.

These rudimentary, fundamental rules are available to preachers who are impassioned to make sermon delivery persuasive. Throughout this chapter, we have acknowledged that we are advocates of sermon discourses that transcend parochial boundaries. We believe that Gardner Taylor's sermon discourses did so, and in addition we believe that Taylor's discourses were persuasive in local congregations, institutional spheres, and the public square. Consequential orators and preachers share the same primary objective: to be understood. Blair provides for us an overview for preachers to take into consideration:

> The great objects which every public speaker will naturally have in his eye in forming his delivery are, first, to speak so as to be fully and easily understood by all who hear him; and next, to speak with grace and force, so as to please and to move his audience. Let us consider what is most important with respect to each of these. In order to be fully and easily understood, the four chief requisites are, due degree of loudness of voice; distinctness; slowness; and propriety of pronunciation.[19]

What Blair refers to as requisites we make known as traits that enhance delivery. Taylor's sermon "Preaching in an Urban Situation" is an example of how these traits function in real space and time.

Managing One's Voice and Physical Presence

Let us add, Taylor mastered these traits—he knew how to use his voice, to pronounce his words with scrupulous diction in cadence and with a deliberate pace. At times, his baritone voice sounded like a whisper; at other times, he sounded like a peal of thunder echoing after lightning has struck the earth. In short, Taylor mastered all the traits of a speakerly tone. Speakerly tone, we suggest, is similar to what Blair called the three pitches of the human voice—low, middle, and high pitches:

> Much depends for this purpose on the proper pitch, and management of the voice. Every man has three pitches in his voice; the High, the Middle, and the Low one. The High is that which he uses in calling aloud to someone at a distance. The Low is when he approaches to whisper. The Middle is that which he employs in common conversation, and which he should generally use in Public Discourse. For it is a great mistake, to imagine that one must take the highest pitch of his voice, in order to be well heard by a great assembly.[20]

Blair's management of voice pitch is important. There are similar views shared between Blair and Henry Ward Beecher, a prince of the nineteenth-century American pulpit. During his Yale lectures on preaching, Beecher gave considerable attention to what may be called various vocal elements:

> If a man can be taught in the beginning of his ministry something about the suppleness of voice and the method of using it, it is very much to his advantage. For example, I have known scores of preachers who had not the slightest knowledge of the explosive tones of the voice. Now and then a man falls into it "by nature," as it is said: that is, he stumbles into it accidentally. But the acquired power of raising the voice again in its higher keys, and the knowledge of its possibilities under these different phases, will be very helpful. It will help the preacher to spare both himself and his people. It will help him to accomplish results almost unconsciously, when it has become a habit, that could not be gained in any other way.[21]

Beecher was a proponent of voice preparation and diligent voice drill. He cautioned, however, and we agree, if voice training can result in an unconscious effort, a natural behavior, it will be helpful to some. There was a time, Gardner Taylor admits, when "I wanted to take elocution and to train my voice, my wife discouraged me from it, [and] so, I never did it. Her reasoning was that preaching never ought to be a finished thing, a polished performance. She was right."[22]

We suggest that a pulpiteer's physical presence is an attraction or a distraction; this greatly depends on the preacher's attention to her or his posture. This indicates a preacher's self-assurance, competence, confidence, and ethical courage:

> It is not necessary that a man should stand awkwardly because it is natural. It is not necessary that a man, because he may not be able to stand like a statue of Apollo, should stand ungracefully. He loses, unconsciously, a certain power; for, although he does not need a very fine physical figure (which is rather a hindrance, I think), yet he should be pleasing in his bearing and gestures.[23]

Of course, a preacher's gestures are a part of her or his physical presence. We acknowledge that most people are visual and we are critiqued and measured, if not biasedly judged, by our physical presence. Our physical presence can intimidate some, and we cannot change this. However, we must be aware that our bodily presence can conjure unintended perceptions, as Frederick Douglass knew well:

> For African American orators who spoke before predominately white or biracial audiences, this process of claiming the authority to name racial difference took on an added significance. Their presence on the platform would evoke for antebellum audiences the connotations of physical difference, particularly the claims that such distinctions were proof of inferiority. The reports of Douglass's lectures, for example, frequently refer to his body quite explicitly, revealing, as Robert Fanuzzi notes, that white audiences considered "the physique of the black orator" a public spectacle.[24]

We concede that persons who speak in cross-cultural settings will experience inevitable skepticism and derision. Those who speak to persuade institutional spheres and the public square to embrace ethical possibilities will face defamation of character in a fashion similar to that of Douglass.

Unfortunately, some will face gender and racial indifferences, while still others will receive unwarranted projected transference of inferiority. Nevertheless, study, preparation, practice, discipline, and an awareness of voice pitch, gestures, and posture are beneficial and will win out more than they repel and lose. All of this is a part of the platform speaker's and preacher's way of life. What follows is a closer observation of Taylor's use of his voice to aid him in sermon delivery. Blair defines voice management as high, middle, and low pitch. There are variations in the ways that words can be manipulated for a dramatic effect, while still there are other ways to manipulate words that provide a perception of warmth and gravitas.

There remains a keen interest in Taylor's ability to manipulate words, for example, how he was able to clearly pronounce words just above a whisper. Often in his sermon introductions, his speakerly tone was pedestrian. We could hear and see him thinking aloud. He spoke with warmth and gravitas. His sermon introductions were nonthreatening, even though he possessed a regal baritone voice. In an earlier chapter, we indicated that Taylor often used a protracted introduction. His introductions are effective in part because Taylor uses his sermon introductions as a way to draw an audience into his narrative. One writer has thought about how Taylor would gain intimacy with his audience's attention:

> Gardner Taylor begins by picking a word, such as reconciliation or communion, or sisterhood. First he just says it, but then you can see him warming up to it. Clearly he loves that word and he is going to do wonderful things for it and to it. He tries just rolling it out of this mouth; then, staccato-like he bounces it around a bit; he starts to take it apart, piece by piece, and then put it together in different ways. And pretty soon you have a lot of people engaged in wondering and puzzling with Dr. Taylor, trying to figure out what this word and idea of reconciliation is all about. They walk around the word, looking at it from different angles. Taylor gets on top of it, and looks down, then he lifts up a corner and peeks underneath; you can see this is going to be a difficult word to get to know. He whispers it and then he shouts it; he pats, pinches, and probes it; and then he pronounces himself unsatisfied, and all the people disagree. "It's time to look at what the great apostle Paul has to say about this here word reconciliation." And all the people agree.[25]

This parallels our view. We hold that Taylor's low voice pitch is akin to a stage actor performing a soliloquy. At times, Taylor seems be having a conversation with himself. Often Taylor began his sermons in a low pitch in which he pronounced his words in a slow and exaggerated pace, and again, he does it just above a whisper.

An example of Taylor's voice modulated in a low pitch is located in "Preaching in the Urban Situation." Also take notice of Taylor's ability to make his narrative descriptive and detailed; his narrative then becomes a living word picture.

> If one turns to the Gospel of John the tenderness with which Jesus holds these men immediately leaps up almost out of the pages: "Abide in me and I in you. No more have I called you servants," and on and on (based on John 15). And then those infinitely rallying words that have meant so much to so many people when the strange and eerie hush of death has come into their homes: "Let not your heart be troubled" (John 14:1, 27).[26]

> The pouring of the wine, the breaking of the bread, there is something endlessly tender about that, infinitely personal and intimate. And this part of religion we get, and this part cannot be left out, cannot be forgotten, cannot be abandoned. Without it, those deep interior transactions, there is no faith. Those moments when heaven comes down our souls to greet, and glory crowns the mercy seat. This is vital to the Christian life.[27]

These words cannot be delivered effectively in a high or middle pitch. These words depict that a conversation is taking place; it is taking place in a whisper. It is a soliloquy: "tenderness, abide . . . No more . . . I call you servants . . . strange and eerie hush of death has come . . . Let not your heart be troubled." These words cannot be uttered persuasively without the person who is speaking these words; she or he is feeling deeply what they are emoting: "there is something endlessly tender . . . infinitely personal and intimate."

Taylor's ponderous stutter is on display in the following long excerpt. We concede that reading Taylor does not capture his eloquence and style that galvanizes audiences. The printed word does not fully recreate his voice in action in sermon delivery. Still, we can maintain that Taylor's speakerly tone is a demonstration of a middle pitch:

> We have come now to the end of the decade of the 1960s. You remember how it all began. This decade began on that chill morning, on that windswept day in the nation's capital with a man, about whom they said he walked like a prince and talked like a poet, standing before

not only the assembled throng who'd gathered for the inauguration but before the television cameras and therefore before the nation. He spoke to this country about having given up some of its noblest purposes and destiny. And then, uttering those words that somehow spoke to some slumbering gallantry in the nation's heart, President Kennedy said, "Ask not what your country can do for you, but what you can do for your country." The new president spoke eloquently about how sadly, how tragically the country had slipped from its highest purposes. There was some impending crisis waiting upon the nation, to use one writer's words, "still a crisis not yet defined, still locked in the womb of time, but stirring uncomfortably like an embryo, its face not yet known." Even before that, the retiring president had summoned a commission and the Congress had put its seal upon it to examine the national purpose, because there was some disease in this country, a kind of moral flabbiness and a sort of purposelessness which had settled upon the land.[28]

Taylor's middle pitch can be identified through his word choice, which is an integral aspect of the art of delivery. Taylor's word choice points to his voice's elevation. What is more, his speakerly tone rises: "this decade began on that chill morning, on that windswept day in the nation's capital with a man, about whom they said he walked like a prince and talked like a poet." He continues, "There was some impending crisis waiting upon the nation, . . . 'still a crisis not yet defined, still locked in the womb of time, but stirring uncomfortably like an embryo, its face not yet known.'" These words are Emerson-like, transcendental. Taylor's words then are a burst into the sublime. Taylor's sublimity adds an eloquent affect to his art of delivery, but it is effective only when these words are delivered in a middle-pitch, speakerly tone.

This final example is an excerpt that depicts Taylor's speakerly tone in high pitch. With a close reading, we can hear Taylor's frustration with the nation's recalcitrant and stubborn indifference to the 1960s violence. We suggest that Taylor is speaking in a high pitch, but it is also a voice of lament:

Its stresses now are beginning to try the very heart of the republic. What was established that Thursday evening and that Friday is forever valid. Only might makes right. That is an angle of vision and thrust of the gospel particularly relevant to this last thirty years of the twentieth century and the beginning of the twenty-first. So it doesn't make much difference when all is said and done, not by that eternal gauge. Finally, it is not up to America as to what will be, what must be. There is another law higher, far more excellent, and if our stance on those battlefields in Asia with strange names is grotesque and wrong before that ultimate gaze, what we say or do down here will make little difference because it cannot come out but one way. Stir the cemetery of history and inquire of the sleeping giants, Babylon, Rome, and Assyria, ask them all, "Does wrong work?" It just does not work. Right makes might![29]

All casual observers can hear the frustration and pessimistic optimism that rises out of Taylor's speakerly tone. He begins his lament with praise and blame: "This country, with all of the incalculable resources, the immeasurable riches, natural and human, and with a political creed among the most hallowed . . . still is a nation torn and divided." He follows with praise and advice: "There is another law higher, far more excellent . . . what we say or do down here will make little difference . . . Stir the cemetery of history and inquire . . . It just does not work. Right makes might!"

Let us remember that words have nearly unlimited power and authority. Words are a human construct as well as a social invention. It should be a preacher's goal to employ her or his words to communicate effectively with an audience. Let us add that words have a psychological effect. Psychologically, words impose on the emotional depths of the human psyche (soul). Preachers, we should be aware of this phenomenon and its influence upon our preaching and more narrowly upon our sermon delivery. Words matter. Time matters. The context for which we preach and deliver those words matter.

Managing Cultural and Congregational Expectations

If a church culture is organized around a twenty-five-minute sermon, we may consider that during our preparation. One minute that we preach beyond that audience's cultural expectation, that extra minute becomes for that audience a psychological barrier. More clearly, denominational expectations are cultural and psychological, as Henry Ward Beecher explains:

> You will find in the Episcopal Church—and I do not say whether it is best or not—that the average duration of the sermon is twenty or twenty-five minutes, the service occupying an hour and a half or two hours, not one eighth of which is occupied in preaching. They depend upon the reading of the Scriptures, upon their musical services, and upon their forms of prayers, the sermon being but a minor thing among many considered more important. On the other hand, churches like the Presbyterians, the Baptist, and the Congregational have no liturgy, and no elaborate church service; they are obliged to emphasize that which they have, and the sermon becomes the chief thing in such denominations. That is the power they hold in their hand, and if they cannot wield that they can wield nothing; for besides that there is very little, I am sorry to say, that is effectual in the work of their ministry, —and that is the weak spot in our scheme.[30]

As was earlier mentioned, Beecher was considered one of the most persuasive and gifted preachers of the nineteenth-century American pulpit. He was an abolitionist who stood squarely and emphatically against legalized, for-profit human bondage. Throngs of people gathered into Brooklyn's Plymouth Church to hear this Christian wordsmith and to witness him deliver his weekly sermon.

Nevertheless, despite Beecher's celebrated oratorical gifts, he cautions the Yale seminarians of 1872 that they should be aware of their denomination's cultural expectations. We must keep in mind there are churches that are organized around certain expectations. These expectations are manifest, realized, and observed in worship. This is a psychological process and expectation, which is another way to say that people hear us emotionally.

Gardner Taylor knew well and thoroughly that church cultures—and we add here, community cultures—are preconditioned and are possessed by their pre-understood cultural expectations. It is critically important for preachers to grasp that sermon delivery is a psychological process. This process includes a psychological clock that sounds the alarm when sermon delivery goes beyond its acceptable length of time. In this sense, time management is an expectation that underscores an audience's temperament. Taylor confirms this argument and uses humor to express it before a group of preachers during an annual conference. Taylor said, "Dr. [Sandy] Ray used to say, and this is a good thing for all of us who preach to remember, that he preached in the right lane because that was where the exits were. That is a tremendous word, to know when to get off. If you do not get through, the people will get through with you."[31]

Taylor reflects how Beecher understands psychological aspects of sermon delivery. We will do well to adhere to those expectations and do the same. Preachers, when we become a part of a particular church and community, must study and learn these expectations. We must learn to craft our sermons in order to meet these expectations.

Understanding Human Nature

Finally, we seek to demonstrate the significance of human nature and how it informs our sermon delivery. That is, if there are denominational, cultural, and psychological expectations, then as preachers we must understand how human nature is a sociopsychological disposition. Aristotle defines these as emotions: Anger, Fear, Hatred, Envy, and Love.[32] Paul of Tarsus defines these in different terms: "But the fruit of the Spirit is love, joy, peace, patience, kindness, goodness, faithfulness, gentleness, and self-control . . . Let us not become conceited, provoking one another, envying one another" (Galatians 5:22-23a,26). In both instances, these positive and negative emotions are a part of the psychology of all audiences, secular and sacred. We take notice, however, that Paul of Tarsus employs the arts of eloquence and style to inform the delivery of his discourse.

Therefore, arts of eloquence, style, and sermon delivery are used to persuade the psychology of human nature or more narrowly the psychology of a particular audience. Plainly stated, there is interrelatedness or an intersection between psychology and human nature. Paradoxically, these impose themselves upon the arts of eloquence, style, and delivery. We restate here that words have nearly unlimited power and authority. We add, words have nearly unlimited power because words affect the human psyche or humanity's nature.

Cooper, among the most brilliant scholars of Aristotelian rhetoric, makes this clear in the following claim:

> The Rhetoric of Aristotle is a practical psychology and the most helpful book extant for writers of prose and for speakers of every sort. Everyone whose business it is to persuade others—lawyers, legislators, statesmen, clergymen, editors, teachers—will find the book useful when it is read with attention. And the modern psychologist commonly will find that he has observed the behavior of human beings less carefully than Aristotle, even though the author keeps reminding us that in the Rhetoric his analysis of thought and conduct is practical, not scientifically precise and complete.[33]

Cooper unmistakably states that rhetoric is a practical psychology, and all know that rhetoric is the art of persuasion. If we play with this for a moment, the art of persuasion is a psychological process. The art of persuasion then is a process that focuses on the psychology of the individual and collective souls of people.

The wordsmith, whether she or he is an editor, teacher, lawyer, or statesmen or stateswomen—and especially a preacher—knows that words, time, and cultural context matter. As Gardner Taylor has said, words or language is the preacher's currency. Those who proclaim these words must remain aware of human nature, its moods, and its emotions—and that there is a pathology that underscores all aspects of the human narrative.

> A speech has its end in persuasion, the speaker or writer must know that nature of the soul he wishes to persuade. That is, he must know human nature, with its ways of reasoning, its habits, desires, and emotions, and must know the kind of argument that will persuade each kind of men, as also the emotional appeal that will gain their assent; every detail, the choice of the individual words and phrases, the arrangement of larger and smaller parts, each single item in the speech is to be determined by its effect upon the soul.[34]

We find this to be informative and a significant help for preachers. We are better prepared to deliver a sermon discourse when we recognize that words have psychological power and authority to persuade. When we make this a part of our study—the elements in a narrative, all kinds of narratives and especially in biblical narratives—we begin to notice the psychological traits that are present in all biblical texts. We suggest strongly that these traits should influence and even persuade the preacher's sermon preparation and delivery.

Conclusion

In order to affect human nature, preachers must use all available tools to persuade an audience to consider our claims. We suggest that preachers can learn from Taylor's art of eloquence, style, and delivery. There is an intersection that exists and is located in his sermon discourse "Preaching in the Urban Situation." Taylor brings his sermon discourse to its close in the following way:

> On that fateful Thursday and Friday, in some deep and unspeakable sense, we know that God got into the heart of it all and took upon himself the ominous entail, the terrible consequence, and turned the tide. It was not something simple and facile like so much of our preaching seems to say: Ah, throw your shoulders back now and lift up your chin. There's something far deeper than that and far more costly. This is the blasphemy in easy preaching. And our kind of shallow, optimistic advice to people fails to see something far deeper and far more costly. This letter of love we've got has blood marks on it. It was a hard fight, a difficult one, and it took all that God had, every bit. And for one terrible, brief, blinding moment it seemed that that was not enough. For if we read this language of imagery of the New Testament, it seems at least for one arctic dreadful moment, for one terribly desolate second, that everything sane in the universe had lost its balance and the awful shimmers up out of the darkness: "My God, my God!" But at the last, as he moved through the river, the word was that it was all safe. "Father, into thy hands," as if that grip had held firm when all of the massive concentrated power of hell's grip had slipped. They sang a hymn and went out.
>
> That is what the gospel is about in the latter part of the twentieth century. Every strength to your arm and heart and spirit as you make ready to preach it.[35]

Taylor's sermon conclusion soars among the eagles. He summarizes his discourse's entirety in a single pregnant paragraph. He began,

"On that fateful Thursday and Friday." He then repeats and reinforces his pessimistic optimism: "God got into the heart of it all and took upon himself the ominous entail, the terrible consequence, and turned the tide." Once again we locate Taylor's praise and blame and praise and advice, which are interrelated: "like so much of our preaching seems to say: Ah, throw your shoulders back now and lift up your chin. There's something far deeper than that and far more costly. This is the blasphemy in easy preaching. And our kind of shallow, optimistic advice to people fails to see something far deeper and far more costly." This is an exemplary example of how Taylor epitomizes the arts of eloquence, style, and delivery.

Finally, he answers his own rhetorical question that was presented to the privileged faculty and students. We recall, "What is the angle and vision and thrust of the gospel that is particularly and peculiarly relevant for that generation to which you will be addressing the gospel of Jesus Christ?" Then Taylor answered, "But at the last . . . the word was that it was all safe. 'Father, into thy hands,' as if that grip had held firm when all of the massive concentrated power of hell's grip had slipped. They sang a hymn and went out. That is what the gospel is about in the latter part of the twentieth century. Every strength to your arm and heart and spirit as you make ready to preach it."

Epigraphs

Richard Lischer, ed., *The Company of Preachers: Wisdom on Preaching, Augustine to the Present* (Grand Rapids, MI: Eerdmans, 2002), 104.

Gardner C. Taylor, "Preaching in the Urban Situation," in *The Words of Gardner Taylor*, comp. Edward L. Taylor, vol. 5: *Lectures, Essays, and Interviews* (Valley Forge, PA: Judson Press, 2001), 89.

NOTES

1. Lane Cooper, *The Rhetoric of Aristotle* (Englewood Cliffs, NJ: Prentice Hall, 1960), 18.

For these three kinds of Rhetoric there are also three several ends. (1) The aim of the deliberative speaker concerns advantage and injury; for the one who exhorts recommends a course of action as better, and one who dissuades deters us from it as worse; other considerations—of

THE ART OF ELOQUENCE

justice and injustice, or honor and dishonor—he makes subsidiary to this end [of the expedient]. (2) The aim of judicial pleaders concerns justice and injustice, and they in like manner make the other considerations subsidiary to these. (3) The aim of those who praise and blame concerns honor and dishonor, and such speakers likewise subordinate the other considerations to these.

4. Ibid., 53.

5. Edward P. J. Corbett and Robert J. Connors, *Classical Rhetoric for the Modern Student*, 4th ed. (Oxford: Oxford University Press, 1999), 22.

6. Gardner C. Taylor, "Preaching in the Urban Situation," in *The Words of Gardner Taylor*, comp. Edward L. Taylor, vol. 5: *Lectures, Essays, and Interviews*, 89.

7. Ibid.

8. Charles Reynolds Brown, *The Art of Preaching: The Forty-Eighth Series of Lyman Beecher Lectures on Preaching in Yale University* (New York: Macmillan, 1922), 167–68.

9. Gardner C. Taylor, "Interview with Gardner C. Taylor," in *The Words of Gardner Taylor*, comp. Edward L. Taylor, vol. 5: *Lectures, Essays, and Interviews* (Valley Forge, PA: Judson Press, 2001), 285, 286.

10. Hugh Blair, *Lectures on Rhetoric and Belles Lettres*, ed. Linda Ferreira-Buckley and S. Michael Halloran, Landmarks in Rhetoric and Public Address (1783; Carbondale: Southern Illinois University Press, 2005), 269.

11. Michael Eric Dyson, "Gardner Taylor: Poet Laureate of the Pulpit," *Christian Century* (January 4-11, 1995), 14. Dyson writes that "though Taylor has combined both approaches—he was active in the civil rights movement in New York, and was a close friend and preaching idol of Martin Luther King Jr.—he realizes that his life work has ruled out the kind of visibility that comes from high-profile activism. [Taylor said], 'I recognized early that the work I do is not attention grabbing.'"

12. Blair, *Lectures on Rhetoric and Belles Lettres*, 197.

13. Taylor, "Interview with Gardner C. Taylor," 284, 286.

14. Cleophus J. LaRue, *Rethinking Celebration: From Rhetoric to Praise in African American Preaching* (Louisville, KY: Westminster John Knox Press, 2016), ix.

15. Ibid., ix.

16. Hugh Blair, "Eloquence of the Pulpit," in *Lectures on Rhetoric and Belles Lettres*, ed. Linda Ferreira-Buckley and S. Michael Halloran, Land-

marks in Rhetoric and Public Address (1783; Carbondale: Southern Illinois University Press, 2005), 317.

17. Ibid.

18. LaRue, *Rethinking Celebration*, x. LaRue adds this excerpt from Neil Postman, *Amusing Ourselves to Death: Public Discourse in the Age of Show Business* (New York: Penguin Books, 1985), 27–28.

> The decline of a print-based epistemology and the accompanying rise of a television-based epistemology has had grave consequences for public life, that we are getting sillier by the minute . . . As typography moves to the periphery of our culture and television takes its place at the center, the seriousness, clarity, and above all, value of public discourse dangerously declines.

19. Blair, *Lectures on Rhetoric and Belles Lettres*, 369.

20. Ibid.

21. Henry Ward Beecher, *Yale Lectures on Preaching* (New York: J. B. Ford and Company, 1872), 130.

22. Edward Gilbreath, "The Pulpit King: The Passion and Eloquence of Gardner Taylor, a Legend among Preachers," *Christianity Today* (December 11, 1995), 25–28.

23. Beecher, *Yale Lectures on Preaching*, 136.

24. Jacqueline Bacon, *The Humblest May Stand Forth: Rhetoric, Empowerment and Abolition* (Columbia: University of South Carolina, 2002), 73.

25. Timothy George, "Honor to Whom Honor Is Due," in *Our Sufficiency Is of God: Essays on Preaching in Honor of Gardner C. Taylor*, ed. Timothy George, James Earl Massey, and Robert Smith Jr. (Macon, GA: Mercer University Press, 2010), xxii. Also see Richard John Neuhaus, *Freedom for Ministry* (Grand Rapids, MI: Eerdmans, 1979), 177.

26. Taylor, "Preaching in the Urban Situation," 90.

27. Ibid.

28. Ibid., 93.

29. Ibid., 94–95.

30. Beecher, *Yale Lectures on Preaching*, 107–8.

31. Gardner C. Taylor, "Great Preachers Remembered," in *The Words of Gardner Taylor*, comp. Edward L. Taylor, vol. 5: *Lectures, Essays and Interviews* (Valley Forge, PA: Judson Press, 2001), 113.

32. Cooper, *Rhetoric of Aristotle*, 90–131.

33. Ibid., xvii.

34. Ibid., xx.

35. Taylor, "Preaching in the Urban Situation," 95.

Afterword

Lightning in a Bottle and Peals of Thunder

*I*n his baritone voice, oftentimes we heard him talk about his humble beginnings in the "Louisiana swamp country." It was his watermark, his imprimatur. From Baton Rouge to New York, and to the world, his voice was a clarion call above human pretentiousness and pretenses, noise and distractions. His voice symbolized lightning in a bottle and peals of thunder.

He made choices. He decided where he would stand on sociopolitical issues; his decisions were informed by his theological convictions formed in part by his moral understanding of the world, a world first introduced to him in a certain time and place, surrounded by special people. Near perfect, all of it came together to shape the ethical mind and heart of an orator who would become, perhaps, the twentieth century's greatest preacher of the gospel.

He rose meteorically. From the beginning, he was among the most gifted. He seemed to have avoided the awkwardness that goes along with the majorities who learn how to speak publicly. His photographic memory may have aided him—one of the surest gifts afforded to the platform speaker. His pulpit presence cannot be taught. In this way, he is among the company of Frederick Douglass, Mordecai Wyatt Johnson, and Vernon Johns. These gifts and so many more were always there.

He studied. He nurtured his craft. Though he read broadly, he seemed to find his voice among the Victorian preachers. These preachers practiced, participated in, and perfected what is often called the elocutionary movement. Of the movement, he was attracted to the Scottish preachers and their use of language. He mastered it. Their spoken and written composition—he mastered it. Like the Scottish preachers, he too kept presence and participation in the academy. He practiced. He taught. He gave the Lyman Beecher and Mullins lectures.

He felt (June 18, 1918–April 5, 2015). He did not lose his common touch. He remembered the least of these. He moved among ostracized people in a similar manner as he moved among the elites. This is what his watermark means, his "Louisiana swamp country." Through this lens, he identified preachers who he believed had his similar gifts, ambitions, and disciplines. He mentored them. No one who heard him laugh, witnessed his wit, his twinkling eyes, his smile, his genius could deny his genuine warmness. No one who heard him preach will forget his sheer power: his power to capture lightning in a bottle, his powerful voice like thunder. We heard it peal, and we hear it echo.

This afterword is adapted from a memorial originally published by New Baptist Covenant, November 1, 2016, http://newbaptistcovenant .org/lightning-in-a-bottle-and-peals-of-thunder/.

Index